POCKET NATURE
TREES

POCKET NATURE
TREES

ALLEN COOMBES

DORLING KINDERSLEY

LONDON, NEW YORK, MUNICH,
MELBOURNE, AND DELHI

DK LONDON
Senior Art Editor Ina Stradins
Project Art Editor Vanessa Thompson
Senior Editor Angeles Gavira
Editor Georgina Garner
DTP Designer Adam Shepherd
Picture Editor Neil Fletcher
Illustrator Gill Tomblin
Production Controllers
Elizabeth Cherry, Melanie Dowland
Managing Art Editor Phil Ormerod
Managing Editor Liz Wheeler
Art Director Bryn Walls
Category Publisher Jonathan Metcalf

DK DELHI
Designers Supriya Sahai,
Shefali Upadhyay, Kavita Dutta
Editors Glenda Fernandes,
Sheema Mookherjee, Dipali Singh
Editorial Consultant Anita Roy
Editorial Support Chumki Sen,
Bhavna Seth
DTP Designers Sunil Sharma,
Balwant Singh, Jessica Subramanian
DTP Co-ordinator Pankaj Sharma
Managing Art Editor Aparna Sharma

This edition published in 2010
First published in Great Britain in 2004 by
Dorling Kindersley Limited
80 Strand, London WC2R 0RL

A Penguin Company

Copyright © 2004
Dorling Kindersley Limited

ISBN 978 1 4053 4998 7

Reproduced by Colourscan, Singapore
Printed and bound by Sheck Wah Tong, China

see our complete catalogue at
www.dk.com

CONTENTS

a million voices for nature

The Royal Society for the Protection of Birds (RSPB) speaks out for birds and wildlife, tackling the problems that threaten our environment. It works with bird and habitat conservation organizations in a global partnership called BirdLife International. Nature is amazing – help us keep it that way.

THE AUTHOR

Allen Coombes is a botanist at the Sir Harold Hillier Gardens and the author of several books on trees.

How this book works

This guide covers over 300 of the most commonly seen tree species in Europe. At the beginning of the book is a short introduction which focuses on the process of identification in the field. The trees are then divided into four easily recognized groups: Conifers with Needles, Conifers with Scales, Broadleaved Simple, Broadleaved Compound. Within each group, the trees are arranged by family and by genus so that similar looking species appear together for ease of comparison.

SCIENTIFIC NAME

▽ GROUP INTRODUCTIONS
Each of the four chapters opens with an introductory page describing the group's shared characteristics. Photographs of representative species show the diversity in the group.

CORNER PICTURE
Provides a view of one of the characteristic features of the tree, seen in situ.

CORNER CAPTION
Describes the feature pictured above, adding to the information provided in the main description.

DETAIL PICTURES
These tinted boxes show individual parts of the tree in greater detail, and may include leaves, flowers, or fruit.

SCALE DRAWING
To give an indication of the plant's height, a scaled drawing of the tree is set next to a drawing of an adult human. See panel above right.

1

H
Qu

Th
Its
lar
an
the
inc
sta
2cr
the

leaf
long

DEEPLY lobed leaves are clustered towards the end of the shoots, and turn yellow-brown in autumn.

notched, larger lobe

male catkin

HEIGHT *30m.*
SPREAD *25m.*
BARK *Dark grey, rugged, ar fissured.*
FLOWERING TIME *Late spr*
OCCURRENCE *Woodland, in*
SIMILAR SPECIES *None – i*
leaves make it highly distinc

Conifers with Needles

This widely distributed group contains many of the most familiar conifers. Most are evergreen, such as the pines, firs, spruces, and cedars but there are a few deciduous examples, such as the larches. The evergreens usually have leathery leaves marked with white lines or pores on one side, both features that help them to reduce water loss. The Scots Pine (pictured) is one of the best known examples of this group.

▷ SINGLE-PAGE ENTRIES
Species that exhibit greater or more complex features, or are of special interest, are given a full page.

BROADLEAVED SIMPLE **201**

White Willow
Salix alba (Salicaceae)

The common large waterside willow of Europe, White Willow is a vigorous, spreading, deciduous tree, often with drooping shoots. The slender, lance-shaped, finely toothed leaves end in long, tapered points. They are silky and hairy when young, becoming dark green above and blue-green below. The tiny flowers are borne in small catkins as the leaves emerge; the males are yellow while the females are green and are borne on separate trees.

LONG, narrow leaves show their blue-green undersides with the slightest movement. Breezy days the orchard.

spreading habit

drooping branches

GREY-BROWN, the bark can be corky in some forms, a feature inherited from the Cork Oak.

NOTES
Describe striking or unique physical features that will help you identify the species, or provide other interesting background information.

L

Qu

A h
this
sha
glo
The
ar

The White Willow is often cultivated to encourage the growth of strong shoots; the wood of these shoots can be used as a source of fuel or in basket making, or for making cricket bats.

HEIGHT *25m.* SPREAD *20m.*
BARK *Grey-brown, deeply fissured with age.*
FLOWERING TIME *Spring.*
OCCURRENCE *Riversides and important all over Europe and commonly planted.*
SIMILAR SPECIES *Crack Willow (Salix fragilis), which has slightly larger leaves that start dropping to catch hairs; Cricket Willow (s.333), which has bright green, smooth leaves, and shoots that snap with each.*

▽ SPECIES ENTRIES

The typical page describes two species. Each entry follows the same easy-to-access structure. All have one main photograph of the species, which is taken in the plant's natural setting in the wild. This is supported by one or more detail pictures that show the individual parts of the tree in close-up. Annotations, scale artworks, and a data box add key information and complete the entry.

SCALE MEASUREMENTS

Two small scale drawings are placed next to each other in every entry as a rough indication of tree size. The figure represents a 6-ft human. The tree illustration represents the tree at maturity in the wild. Bare branches on one side mean the tree is deciduous; full foliage means the tree is evergreen.

Tree height
20m

Human figure represents a height of 1.8m (6ft)

CHAPTER HEADING

EAVED SIMPLE

rian Oak

to (Fagaceae)

uous tree has stout, slightly hairy shoots.
have numerous blunt-tipped lobes, the
times notched, and are dark green above
eneath. The flowers are borne in catkins;
-green and pendulous, the females
The short-
p to
in

broadly
spreading habit

be Oak

anica (Fagaceae)

n Turkey Oak (p.134) and Cork Oak (p.143),
ergreen tree. Its leaves are very variable in
and are edged with pointed teeth. They are
n above and grey-white with hairs beneath.
borne in catkins, the males yellow-green
, the females inconspicuous. Acorns
cm long, in cups covered by
bristly scales, ripen in
the second year.

rounded
top

leaf to
12cm
long

HEIGHT 30m. **SPREAD** 30m.
BARK Grey-brown, fissured, sometimes corky.
FLOWERING TIME Late spring.
OCCURRENCE Woodland, usually with parent
species; commonly cultivated, native to
S. Europe.
SIMILAR SPECIES Turkey Oak (p.134),
Cork Oak (p.143).

COMMON NAME

Some species do not have an English common name. In these cases the scientific name is given as the entry heading.

FAMILY NAME

The botanical family name is given in brackets after the scientific name. Where opinions differ, more than one name may be listed.

DESCRIPTION

Conveys the main features and distinguishing characteristics of the species.

ANNOTATION

Characteristic features of the species are picked out in the annotation.

PHOTOGRAPHS

Illustrate the tree in its natural setting.

COLOUR BANDS

Bands are colour-coded, with a different colour for each of the four chapters.

OTHER KEY INFORMATION

These coloured panels provide consistent information on the following points:
HEIGHT: *the tree's height in the wild.*
SPREAD: *the width of the tree in the wild.*
FLOWERING TIME: *the season in which the tree produces flowers.*
OCCURRENCE: *the habitat in which the tree can be found and its geographic distribution. Some trees are not native to Europe and may only be found in cultivation in the region. In these instances the species' native origin is also given.*
SIMILAR SPECIES: *lists species that look similar to the one featured, often providing a distinguishing feature to help tell them apart. Species not profiled in this book may be listed, in which case a distinguishing feature is always given.*

Identification

Trees have many characters that can be used to identify them, some obvious, some less so. Note the shape of the tree and where and when it is growing, but also study closely the leaves, flowers, fruit, and bark. Remember that most plants are variable and features such as leaves can differ in size and shape, even on the same tree.

Leaf Shape

Tree leaves are extremely diverse. Check if the leaf is simple (one individual blade) or compound (divided into leaflets) and how any leaflets are arranged (pinnately or palmately, for example). Assess the shape and size of all its elements.

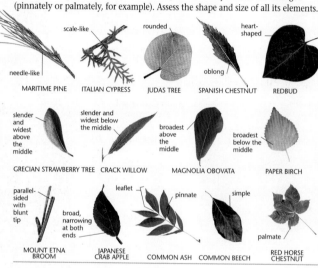

needle-like
scale-like
MARITIME PINE
ITALIAN CYPRESS

rounded
JUDAS TREE

heart-shaped
oblong
SPANISH CHESTNUT

REDBUD

slender and widest above the middle
GRECIAN STRAWBERRY TREE

slender and widest below the middle
CRACK WILLOW

broadest above the middle
MAGNOLIA OBOVATA

broadest below the middle
PAPER BIRCH

parallel-sided with blunt tip
MOUNT ETNA BROOM

broad, narrowing at both ends
leaflet
JAPANESE CRAB APPLE

pinnate
COMMON ASH

simple
COMMON BEECH

palmate
RED HORSE CHESTNUT

Leaf Colour and Markings

Leaf colour and markings vary both between and within species. Some leaves change colour as they mature, or just before they fall in autumn; some leaves are marked with prominent veins or are variegated, consisting of patches of colour.

autumn red
RED MAPLE

white line on under-side
GIANT FIR

green upperside
silver green underside
SILVER MAPLE

young leaves bronze-green
older leaves
SPRING CHERRY

prominent veins
RAULI

variegated
NORWAY MAPLE

Leaf Margin and Texture

The leaf margin can vary from untoothed to wavy, toothed, spiny, or variously lobed, depending on the species. Look at them, but also touch and smell the leaves. Plant parts can be characteristically rough, hairy, or scented. For example, evergreens usually have rather leathery leaves while some species of poplar may be hairy or downy on one or both sides.

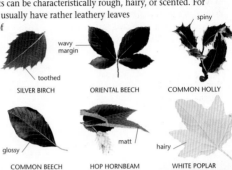

spiny

wavy margin

toothed

SILVER BIRCH

ORIENTAL BEECH

COMMON HOLLY

lobed

glossy

matt

hairy

PYRENEAN OAK

COMMON BEECH

HOP HORNBEAM

WHITE POPLAR

Leaf Arrangement

Leaf arrangement can provide clues to a tree's identity. All maples and ashes, for example, have leaves that grown opposite one another, while oak leaves are alternate and sometimes in a cluster towards the ends of the shoots.

opposite

clustered

alternate

DOWNY OAK

MOOSEWOOD

HUNGARIAN OAK

irregular sprays

flattened sprays

LAWSON CYPRESS

ITALIAN CYPRESS

whorls

ATLAS CEDAR

Flowers

Note their size, colour, and form, but also consider how and where flowers are borne on the plant. Some trees may have separate male and female flowers, on the same or on different plants.

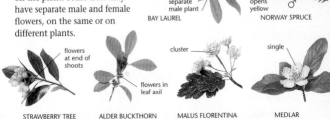

female plant ♀

♀

female opens red

separate male plant ♂

BAY LAUREL

male opens yellow ♂

NORWAY SPRUCE

flowers at end of shoots

flowers in leaf axil

cluster

single

STRAWBERRY TREE

ALDER BUCKTHORN

MALUS FLORENTINA

MEDLAR

Fruit

While different types of cone help to distinguish conifers, other trees bear very different forms of fruit, including fleshy, characteristically coloured berries, hard-shelled nuts, and flattened pods. Fruits protect the tree's seeds and facilitate seed distribution; some fruits have wings to aid wind-borne dispersal. Even fruits that have fallen to the ground can help identification.

egg-shaped cones
AUSTRIAN PINE

single upright cone
SPANISH FIR

contains multiple seeds
CULTIVATED APPLE

contains single seeds
CHERRY LAUREL

acorn in cup
green husk
ENGLISH OAK

hard shell
BLACK WALNUT

WALNUT

enclosed in bracts
HORNBEAM

woody husk
ORIENTAL BEECH

cylindrical pods
CAROB

small and woody
RED GUM

broad wings
PAPERBARK MAPLE

Silver Fir
Oriental Spruce

FALLEN FRUIT
These cones look similar, but spruce cones fall from the tree intact while fir cones break up on the tree.

DIFFERENT FRUITS
When not in bloom, the Indian Horse Chestnut and the Red Horse Chestnut appear similar, until you observe their very different fruit.

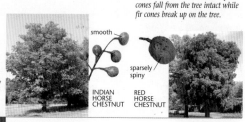

smooth
INDIAN HORSE CHESTNUT

sparsely spiny
RED HORSE CHESTNUT

Habit

Observing a tree's shape, or habit, can help species identification, but be aware that shape can vary greatly: a tree growing in the open will differ in shape to one of the same species growing in a dense forest. Age can also affect the shape of a tree. Take note of all external factors.

COLUMNAR
The Incense Cedar is taller than it is wide.

SPREADING
Many evergreen trees, like this Cretan Maple, are spreading in habit.

CONICAL
Like most young conifers, this Norway Spruce is conical.

SHRUB-LIKE
This exposed Phoenician Juniper grows as a shrub.

Bark

As a tree grows, its trunk expands causing the exterior layers of dead bark to peel or crack. This expansion creates various characteristic bark patterns; it also produces colour and textural differences between young and old specimens. Some trees, such as the Tibetan Cherry, have very distinctive bark colour.

GREY BIRCH   WINGNUT   JAPANESE CEDAR   HIMALAYAN BIRCH   SMOOTH ARIZONA CYPRESS

DATE PLUM   SILVER BIRCH   TIBETAN CHERRY   GREY-BUDDED SNAKE-BARK MAPLE

Seasons

Flowering time and leaf persistence can be defining features for a tree. Deciduous trees lose their leaves in autumn but evergreens retain them, at least until the following season's leaves open. A tree may produce its flowers before its leaves open; another similar-looking tree may flower only after the young leaves are produced.

NORWAY MAPLE

SYCAMORE

HOLM OAK   TURKEY OAK

SEASONALITY
The Holm Oak is evergreen while its cousin the Turkey Oak is deciduous.

FLOWERING
The Norway Maple flowers before its leaves appear; the Sycamore flowers open later.

Habitat

Some trees are naturally widespread but others, due to their preference for specific environmental conditions, may be confined to certain habitats and particular geographical regions. Tree species found in a lowland valley are likely to be very different to those found high in the mountains.

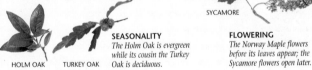

RIVERBANKS
The Alder tree is likely to be found by rivers and in other wet areas.

COASTLINES
The Aleppo Pine is native to the slopes of the Mediterranean coast.

MOUNTAINS
Conifers, such as the Bosnian Pine, thrive in mountainous regions.

Conifers with Needles

This widely distributed group contains many of the most familiar conifers. Most are evergreen, such as the pines, firs, spruces, and cedars but there are a few deciduous examples, such as the larches. The evergreens usually have leathery leaves marked with white lines of pores on one side, both features that help them to reduce water loss. The Aleppo Pine (pictured) is an example found on the Mediterranean coast.

GIANT FIR

SUBALPINE FIR

KOREAN FIR

CALIFORNIA REDWOOD

Maidenhair Tree

Ginkgo biloba (Ginkgoaceae)

The only survivor of an ancient group of trees widespread before the conifers, Maidenhair Tree has distinctive notched leaves borne on slender stalks. The long shoots bear single leaves while the short side shoots bear leaf clusters. The flowers of this deciduous tree are small and yellow-green; males are in catkin-like clusters and females are single or in pairs. Female trees produce fleshy, plum-like seeds with edible kernels. The rotting fruit has a particularly unpleasant odour.

MATT GREEN *leaves are fan-shaped with veins radiating from the base; in autumn they turn bright yellow.*

spreading habit

leaf to 7.5cm long

HEIGHT *30m or more.*
SPREAD *20m.*
BARK *Grey-brown and smooth at first, later ridged and fissured.*
FLOWERING TIME *Spring.*
OCCURRENCE *Cultivated (in gardens and city streets); native to China.*
SIMILAR SPECIES *None.*

Monkey Puzzle

Araucaria araucana (Araucariaceae)

Also known as the Chile Pine, this evergreen tree has shoots that are densely covered by oval, glossy dark green leaves ending in sharp points. The cone-like flowers are green but gradually turn brown. Male and female flowers are borne on separate trees – the cylindrical males on side shoots, the rounded females at the ends of the shoots.

rounded top

OVERLAPPING *leaves often remain attached to the trunk for many years.*

male flower cluster

leaf to 5cm long

shoots densely covered with leaves

cone covered by thin scales

HEIGHT *30m.*
SPREAD *15m.*
BARK *Grey and wrinkled.*
FLOWERING TIME *Summer.*
OCCURRENCE *Cultivated; native to S. Chile and S. Argentina.*
SIMILAR SPECIES *None – very distinctive among commonly grown trees.*

Japanese Cedar

Cryptomeria japonica (Cupressaceae)

A conical evergreen, this tree has slender, bright green leaves that are broadest at the base, tapering to a soft point. Male flowers in small yellow-green clusters are borne in the leaf axils, while the females form rounded cones, green at first, ripening to brown.

SLENDER *needles curve forward along the shoot and female cones are borne at the shoot tips.*

leaves arranged spirally

leaf to 1.5cm long

cone to 2cm wide

red-brown, peeling bark

conical habit

slender, bright green leaves

HEIGHT *30m.*
SPREAD *15m.*
BARK *Red-brown, peeling in fibrous strips.*
FLOWERING TIME *Early spring.*
OCCURRENCE *Cultivated; native to Japan.*
SIMILAR SPECIES *Taiwania cryptomerioide, which has similar foliage when young but has more sharply pointed leaves.*

Chinese Fir

Cunninghamia lanceolata (Cupressaceae)

Conical when young, the evergreen Chinese Fir is later columnar. Its bright green leaves, marked with two white bands beneath, have pointed tips, and spread on either side of the shoot. While male flower clusters are yellow-brown, females are yellow-green; both are borne at the ends of the shoots.

ROUNDED *cones to 4cm wide, green ripening to brown, are borne at the end of the shoots.*

leaf to 6cm long

leaves arranged spirally

yellow-brown flower clusters

columnar habit

HEIGHT *25m.*
SPREAD *10m.*
BARK *Red-brown, ridged.*
FLOWERING TIME *Spring.*
OCCURRENCE *Cultivated; native to S. China and Vietnam.*
SIMILAR SPECIES *None – its long, pointed leaves and rounded cones are distinct.*

Common Juniper

Juniperus communis (Cupressaceae)

This evergreen conifer is of variable habit, from bushy and spreading, to upright and tree-like. Its sharp-pointed needles are glossy green on both surfaces, marked with a broad white band on the upper surface, and arranged in whorls of three on the shoots. The flowers are very small; males are yellow and females green, growing in clusters on separate plants. Female plants bear fleshy, blue-black berry-like cones up to 6mm long, covered at first with a white bloom. Many selections are grown in gardens and the creeping *J. communis var. montana* is common in Arctic and alpine regions.

PROSTRATE *and creeping, or a bushy shrub, or sometimes a tree, this species is of very variable habit.*

glossy green needles

bushy, spreading habit

cone to 6mm long

leaf to 1.2cm long

HEIGHT *6m.*
SPREAD *1–3m.*
BARK *Red-brown with longitudinal ridges; peeling in vertical strips.*
FLOWERING TIME *Spring.*
OCCURRENCE *Heaths and chalky hills throughout Europe.*
SIMILAR SPECIES *Prickly Juniper (p.16), which has leaves with two white bands above and red-brown fruit; it is much more common in S. Europe than the Common Juniper.*

NOTE

This is the only juniper native to N. Europe. The fruit takes two years to ripen, and is found at any time of the year.

Syrian Juniper

Juniperus drupacea (Cupressaceae)

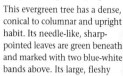

This evergreen tree has a dense, conical to columnar and upright habit. Its needle-like, sharp-pointed leaves are green beneath and marked with two blue-white bands above. Its large, fleshy cones, distinct among junipers, are green and bloomy at first, ripening to purple-black.

ORANGE-BROWN *in colour, the bark of this species, like that of many junipers, peels in thin, vertical strips.*

conical crown

glossy green foliage

cone to 2.5cm long

leaf to 2.5cm long

HEIGHT *15m.* **SPREAD** *3m.*
BARK *Orange-brown, peeling in thin strips.*
FLOWERING TIME *Spring.*
OCCURRENCE *Dry hillsides in S. Greece.*
SIMILAR SPECIES *Common Juniper (p.15), which has similar flowers; other needle-leaved junipers (Juniperus), which have smaller cones.*

Prickly Juniper

Juniperus oxycedrus (Cupressaceae)

An evergreen, large shrub or small tree of conical to spreading habit, this juniper has needle-like leaves in whorls of three; they are glossy, dark green beneath and have two blue-white bands on the upper surface. The flowers, borne in clusters, are small; males yellow and females green, on separate plants. Rounded berry-like cones, up to 1.5cm long, turn from red-brown to purple when ripe.

PURPLE *when ripe, the berry-like cones nestle among the whorls of dark green, sharp-pointed leaves.*

conical to spreading habit

leaf to 2.5cm long

slender, prickly leaves

HEIGHT *15m.* **SPREAD** *10m.*
BARK *Red-brown to purple-brown, peeling in long strips.*
FLOWERING TIME *Spring.*
OCCURRENCE *Dry hillsides in S. Europe.*
SIMILAR SPECIES *Common Juniper (p.15), which has shorter leaves, with only one white band on the upper surface.*

Dawn Redwood

Metasequoia glyptostroboides (Taxodiaceae)

A large, deciduous tree, conical in habit, the Dawn Redwood's slender, soft leaves emerge pale green early in the year, but turn dark green later. They are borne on oppositely arranged side shoots that fall in autumn after the leaves turn yellow- to red-brown. The flowers are small, with the males in drooping, catkin-like clusters, and usually found only in areas with hot summers. The green female flowers develop even in the absence of male flowers, producing rounded green cones that ripen to brown.

TURNING *yellow-brown or red-brown before falling in autumn, the leaves are borne on shoots that are themselves deciduous.*

NOTE

The habit, distinctive bark, and the opposite shoots or buds make this tree easily recognizable, even in winter.

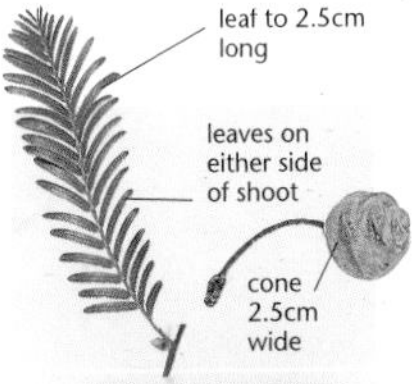

leaf to 2.5cm long

leaves on either side of shoot

cone 2.5cm wide

conical habit

dark green foliage

red-brown bark

HEIGHT *30m.*
SPREAD *10m.*
BARK *Red-brown; peeling in thin strips on mature trees.*
FLOWERING TIME *Early spring.*
OCCURRENCE *Cultivated; native to C. China.*
SIMILAR SPECIES *Swamp Cypress (p.19), which has alternate side shoots, comes into leaf much later, and produces "cypress knees" at the base.*

California Redwood

Sequoia sempervirens (Taxodiaceae)

NEEDLE-SHAPED leaves, with pointed tips, are arranged on both sides of the shoots.

Also known as the Coast Redwood, this evergreen is the world's tallest tree, exceeding 100m in its native habitat. Its dark green leaves are marked with two white bands beneath. The flowers are borne in clusters at the end of the shoots, the male yellow-brown; females green, developing into red-brown, woody cones.

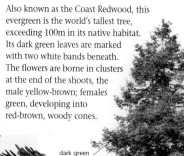

columnar habit

leaves to 2cm long

red-brown cone to 3cm long

dark green foliage

HEIGHT *30–50m.* **SPREAD** *15m.*
BARK *Red-brown, thick, soft, and fibrous.*
FLOWERING TIME *Late winter to early spring.*
OCCURRENCE *Cultivated; native to USA (Oregon and California).*
SIMILAR SPECIES *Giant Redwood (below), which has very different foliage and much larger cones.*

Giant Redwood

Sequoiadendron giganteum (Taxodiaceae)

FIBROUS and rough in texture, the outer bark gives Redwood forests a unique earthy smell.

Variously known as the Big Tree or Wellingtonia, this conical evergreen reaches a massive 80m or more in its native California. The dark green leaves are small and slender, to 8mm long, ending in sharp points, and the foliage is rough to the touch. The flowers are small; the male is yellow, while the green female develops into egg-shaped, woody cones, green at first, later ripening to brown.

yellow male flower

cone to 7.5cm long

conical habit

HEIGHT *30–50m.*
SPREAD *15m.*
BARK *Red-brown, thick, soft, and fibrous.*
FLOWERING TIME *Early spring.*
OCCURRENCE *Cultivated; native to USA (California).*
SIMILAR SPECIES *California Redwood (above), has smaller cones and different foliage.*

Swamp Cypress

Taxodium distichum (Taxodiaceae)

The Swamp or Bald Cypress is conical when young, but becomes columnar with age. Its deciduous shoots are arranged alternately on the branches. The small male flowers hang in catkins up to 20cm long. The green female flowers are found in small clusters at the base of the male catkins and develop into rounded green cones up to 3cm wide, which ripen to brown. When grown near water, trees commonly develop "cypress knees" – woody protuberances that grow vertically from the soil around the tree trunk.

NARROW, *soft, and flattened, the leaves are arranged on either side of the shoots.*

alternate shoots

leaf to 2cm long

leaves arranged on either side of shoot

deciduous foliage

columnar habit

NOTE

The deciduous foliage, as well as the alternate shoots and "cypress knees", (the knee-like bumps on older trees), are distinctive features.

HEIGHT *30m.* **SPREAD** *15m.*
BARK *Grey-brown to red-brown, thin, and rough, peeling in vertical strips; often buttressed at the base.*
FLOWERING TIME *Spring.*
OCCURRENCE *Cultivated; native to S.E. USA.*
SIMILAR SPECIES *Dawn Redwood (p.17), which has leaves on opposite shoots, comes into leaf much earlier, and does not produce "cypress knees".*

Silver Fir

Abies alba (Pinaceae)

This evergreen tree is conical at first, becoming columnar with age. Its shoots have a dense covering of hairs and end in red-brown buds that are not usually sticky. Slender and glossy dark green above, the leaves are marked with two white or greenish white bands beneath. The yellow male flower clusters hang beneath the shoots, while female clusters are green and upright, developing into erect, cylindrical cones with bracts projecting outwards. The ripe cones break up on the tree before falling.

WHITE *or greenish white bands on the undersides of the leaves make them look silvery; the long, flat leaves, notched at the tips, spread outwards on both sides of the shoots.*

pointed crown

glossy, dark green foliage

conical habit, becoming columnar with age

NOTE

One of the commonest firs in European mountains, the Silver Fir is often naturalized and is widely planted for forestry. It is used as a Christmas tree in many parts of Europe.

yellow male flowers

leaf to 3cm long

cone to 15cm long

HEIGHT *50m.* **SPREAD** *15m.*
BARK *Grey and smooth; cracked plates may develop on older trees.*
FLOWERING TIME *Spring.*
OCCURRENCE *Mountain forests, from the Pyrenees and Alps to the Balkan Mountains.*
SIMILAR SPECIES *King Boris Fir (right), which has bolder white markings on the leaves; spruces (Picea), are sometimes confused with firs but have pendulous cones that fall intact.*

King Boris Fir

Abies borisii-regis (Pinaceae)

Possibly of hybrid origin, this conical, evergreen tree has features that are intermediate between the Silver Fir (left) and the Greek Fir (below). Its leaves have two white bands below and are borne on hairy shoots that end in sticky buds. Male flower clusters are yellow; female clusters are green and develop into cylindrical cones up to 15cm long.

SHARPLY *pointed and linear, the glossy, dark green leaves, with white undersides, spread outwards on both sides of the hairy shoots.*

evergreen leaves

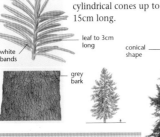

leaf to 3cm long

white bands

conical shape

grey bark

HEIGHT *30m.* **SPREAD** *15m.*
BARK *Grey and smooth; cracks with age.*
FLOWERING TIME *Spring.*
OCCURRENCE *Mountains from Bulgaria to N. Greece.*
SIMILAR SPECIES *Silver Fir (left), which has fainter white bands on its leaves; Greek Fir (below), which has smoother shoots.*

Greek Fir

Abies cephalonica (Pinaceae)

Conical when young, this evergreen tree tends to become columnar with age. Slender, sharp-pointed leaves, with two white bands beneath, are borne on smooth shoots that end in sticky buds. Male flower clusters are yellow, while the female flower clusters are green and develop into upright, cylindrical cones that break up on the tree before falling. The tips of downturned bracts protrude between the cone scales.

BROWN *and upright, the cylindrical cones are 15cm long, narrower at both ends, and have protruding, downturned bracts.*

narrow outline

leaf to 3cm long

whorled, spreading branches

HEIGHT *30m.*
SPREAD *15m.*
BARK *Dark grey and smooth; cracks into plates on older trees.*
FLOWERING TIME *Spring.*
OCCURRENCE *Mountains in Greece.*
SIMILAR SPECIES *King Boris Fir (above), which has hairy shoots.*

Colorado White Fir

Abies concolor (Pinaceae)

Conical when young, this evergreen tree becomes columnar with age. The slender leaves are blue-green to grey-green on both sides with blunt tips. Hanging beneath the shoots, the yellow male flower clusters are red at first; the female clusters are yellow-green and upright, maturing into erect, cylindrical green cones that ripen to brown and then break up on the tree.

LONG, *needle-like, leaves with rounded tips, are upswept above, and spreading beneath, the shoots.*

leaf to 6cm long

male flower cluster

columnar shape

HEIGHT *30m.* **SPREAD** *10m.*
BARK *Grey and smooth on young trees; scaly and ridged with age.*
FLOWERING TIME *Spring.*
OCCURRENCE *Cultivated; native to W. USA and Baja California.*
SIMILAR SPECIES *None – no other species has leaves that are blue-green on both sides.*

Giant Fir

Abies grandis (Pinaceae)

The slender leaves of this fast-growing, large, evergreen tree are bright green above, with two white bands beneath. The leaves are arranged neatly on each side of the shoots. Hanging beneath the shoots are the male flower clusters, which are yellow, or red before they open. The upright, green female flower clusters mature into erect, cylindrical cones. These are green when young, ripening to brown.

SLENDER *leaves spread out in two ranks on either side of the shoots.*

conical habit

2 white bands below leaf

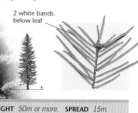

HEIGHT *50m or more.* **SPREAD** *15m.*
BARK *Grey-brown and smooth on young trees; cracks with age.*
FLOWERING TIME *Spring.*
OCCURRENCE *Cultivated (in gardens and for forestry); native to W. North America.*
SIMILAR SPECIES *None – the leaf arrangement is quite distinct.*

Korean Fir

Abies koreana (Pinaceae)

A small, conical, evergreen tree, the Korean Fir has rather short, slender leaves with blunt, sometimes notched tips. They are dark green above, with two broad, silvery white bands beneath. The yellow male flower clusters hang under the shoots and the upright red-purple female flowers ripen to purple. The distinctive, small cones turn brown when mature, later breaking up on the tree.

UPRIGHT *cones, purple when young, are borne in clusters among the shiny, dark green leaves.*

leaf to 2cm long

cone to 7cm long

branches slightly ascending

HEIGHT *10m.*
SPREAD *3m.*
BARK *Dark grey-brown, smooth at first; cracks with age.*
FLOWERING TIME *Spring.*
OCCURRENCE *Cultivated; native to South Korea.*
SIMILAR SPECIES *None.*

Subalpine Fir

Abies lasiocarpa (Pinaceae)

This narrowly conical, evergreen tree becomes columnar when old. Its slender leaves are grey-green, with two white bands beneath and a notched tip. Male flower clusters are yellow, tinged with red before they open. In separate clusters, the females are purple, maturing to upright, cylindrical cones up to 10cm long. These are purple at first, brown when ripe, and break up on the tree.

LONG, *narrow leaves are upright above the shoots, with the central leaves pointing forwards, spreading beneath.*

pointed crown

conical habit becoming columnar with age

leaf to 4cm long

HEIGHT *20m.* **SPREAD** *8m.*
BARK *Grey and smooth, with resin blisters.*
FLOWERING TIME *Spring.*
OCCURRENCE *Cultivated; native to W. North America.*
SIMILAR SPECIES *Noble Fir (p.27), has larger cones; Corkbark Fir (A. lasiocarpa var. arizonica), has bluer leaves and corky bark.*

Sicilian Fir

Abies nebrodensis (Pinaceae)

STOUT *shoots bear the rigid, pointed leaves, cylindrical, dark brown cones, rounded at the apex, and male flower clusters.*

A very rare species, reduced to a few trees in its native habitat, the Sicilian Fir is a broadly, conical, evergreen tree with stout, nearly smooth shoots ending in sticky buds. The rather short, alternate leaves are dark green above with two greenish white bands beneath. Male flower clusters are yellow-green, below the shoots, while females are green and upright, maturing to an upright, cylindrical, cone that breaks up on the tree when ripe.

conical habit

leaf to 1.5cm long

two pale bands beneath

stout, nearly smooth shoots

HEIGHT *15m.*
SPREAD *10m.*
BARK *Orange-brown, cracking with age.*
FLOWERING TIME *Spring.*
OCCURRENCE *Mountain slopes in N. Sicily.*
SIMILAR SPECIES *Silver Fir (p.20), which has longer leaves and lacks the sticky buds on the shoots and is much more widely distributed in the mountains of Europe.*

NOTE

This is the only species of fir native to Sicily, where it has been reduced to a small population by felling and grazing.

Caucasian Fir

Abies nordmanniana (Pinaceae)

This vigorous, evergreen tree is of conical habit. Its alternate, slender leaves are densely arranged; those on the underside of the shoots spread horizontally, those above point forwards. Yellow male flower clusters, which may also be red at first, hang beneath the shoot. The female flower clusters are green and upright, borne separately at the shoot tips. The broadly cylindrical, upright cones are initially green, maturing to purple-brown. They have conspicuous, protruding, downcurved bracts which emerge from between the scales. The cones break up on the tree when ripe.

LINEAR *and notched at the tip, the leaves are glossy and dark green, with two white bands on the lower surface of each needle.*

broadly conical habit

white lines

leaf to 4cm long

yellow male flower cluster

dense, dark green foliage

NOTE

The lush foliage with forward-pointing leaves, and the conspicuous cone bracts, distinguish this species from other firs.

HEIGHT *30m or more.* **SPREAD** *15m.*
BARK *Grey and smooth, cracking into small plates with age.*
FLOWERING TIME *Spring.*
OCCURRENCE *Cultivated (sometimes planted for forestry and grown as a Christmas tree); native to the Caucasus and N.E. Turkey.*
SIMILAR SPECIES *Certain uncommon species such as Greek Fir (p.21) and Noble Fir (p.27) are two of the most similar species; the closely related A. bornmulleriana has smooth shoots.*

Spanish Fir

Abies pinsapo (Pinaceae)

SHORT *and rigid, the grey-green to grey blue leaves are bluntly pointed, standing out all around the shoot.*

A very distinctive, broadly conical, evergreen tree, the Spanish Fir has linear, rigid, grey-green to blue-green leaves. These are densely arranged and stand out all around the smooth shoots; they are sharp-pointed in young plants but blunt in mature ones. Male flowers, borne in clusters on the undersides of the shoots, are red at first, later opening yellow. Borne in separate clusters, the female flowers are green and upright. The cones have pointed tips and ripen from green to brown, finally breaking up on the tree.

dense habit

cone to 15cm long

leaf to 2cm long

male flower cluster

grey-green to blue-green foliage

HEIGHT *20m.* **SPREAD** *10m.*
BARK *Dark grey, smooth, cracking into small, square plates with age.*
FLOWERING TIME *Spring.*
OCCURRENCE *Mountain slopes around Ronda in S. Spain; also planted in the streets.*
SIMILAR SPECIES *The only native fir in its range, it can only be confused with some uncommon relatives found in N. Africa. Also, other firs have leaves spreading either side of the shoot, or at least with a parting above.*

NOTE

The short, rigid leaves arranged around the shoot distinguish this species from other firs; some forms such as 'Glauca' have bluer foliage.

Noble Fir

Abies procera (Pinaceae)

Narrowly conical when young,
the evergreen Noble Fir becomes
columnar with age. The slender,
linear leaves are blue- to grey-
green above, with two silvery
white bands beneath, and
are densely arranged on
hairy shoots, radially above
and spreading to either side
below. Male flower clusters
are red tinged with yellow and
borne on the undersides of the
shoots; female flowers, in
separate clusters, are reddish
or green and upright. The ripe
cones break up on the tree.

tapering
on top

UPRIGHT *brown cones,
up to 25cm long, are
densely covered with
long, downward-
pointing bracts.*

dense
foliage

columnar
habit

leaf to
3cm long

HEIGHT *40m or more.* **SPREAD** *15m.*
BARK *Pale silvery grey, cracking with age.*
FLOWERING TIME *Spring.*
OCCURRENCE *Cultivated in gardens and for
forestry; native to W. USA.*
SIMILAR SPECIES *Other Abies species such
as Subalpine Fir (p.23), have smaller cones
with less conspicuous bracts.*

Atlas Cedar

Cedrus atlantica (Pinaceae)

This evergreen has dark to blue-green leaves that are
slender, needle-like, and to 2cm long. They are borne singly
on long shoots, and in whorls on the
short side shoots. The shoots
have upcurved tips. The male
flower clusters are yellow-
brown and upright. Clusters
of tiny female flowers mature
in one year to barrel-shaped
cones, green at first, ripening
to brown over two to
three years.

BARREL-SHAPED *cones
break up on the tree
once they ripen, before
falling off.*

male flower
cluster to
5cm long

broadly
conical
habit

cone to
8cm long

HEIGHT *30m.* **SPREAD** *20m.*
BARK *Dark grey, cracking into scaly plates
on old trees.*
FLOWERING TIME *Autumn.*
OCCURRENCE *Cultivated; native to the Atlas
Mountains in Algeria and Morocco.*
SIMILAR SPECIES *Cedar of Lebanon (p.28),
which has a flattened and tiered habit.*

Deodar

Cedrus deodara (Pinaceae)

A broadly conical, evergreen tree, the Deodar has larger leaves than other cedars. Green to grey-green, slender, and needle-like, they are borne singly on young shoots and in dense whorls on short side shoots. The upright male flower clusters, to 7cm long, are purple, but turn yellow-brown when open and shedding pollen. The clusters of tiny female flowers mature in one year to barrel-shaped cones.

UPRIGHT, *barrel-shaped cones, green at first, later ripen to purple-brown.*

conical habit

yellow male flower cluster

leaf to 4cm long

cone to 12cm long

HEIGHT *30m.* **SPREAD** *15m.*
BARK *Dark grey; vertical cracks develop with age.*
FLOWERING TIME *Autumn.*
OCCURRENCE *Cultivated; native to the Himalayas, from Afghanistan to Tibet.*
SIMILAR SPECIES *Other cedars (Cedrus), but none has its distinctive nodding shoot tips.*

Cedar of Lebanon

Cedrus libani (Pinaceae)

This evergreen tree is conical when young, but with age develops its characteristic broad head with flattened and tiered branches. The leaves are dark green to grey-green, slender and needle-like, borne singly on long shoots and in dense whorls on short side shoots. The male flower clusters, yellow-brown when open, are upright, to 5cm long. The females are tiny, maturing to brown, barrel-shaped cones.

SPREADING *branches give the tree its distinctive layered appearance.*

cone to 12cm long

flattened branches

leaf to 3cm long

HEIGHT *30m.* **SPREAD** *20m.*
BARK *Dark grey; cracking on older trees.*
FLOWERING TIME *Autumn.*
OCCURRENCE *Cultivated; native to Lebanon, Syria, and Turkey. Replaced in Cyprus by C. brevifolia with shorter leaves and cones.*
SIMILAR SPECIES *Atlas Cedar (p.27), which has upcurved shoot tips.*

European Larch

Larix decidua (Pinaceae)

This fast-growing species is deciduous. Its slender, soft, bright green leaves, each up to 4cm long, open in early spring, turning yellow in autumn. They are arranged singly on distinctive, long yellow shoots but are borne in dense whorls on short side shoots. Male flower clusters, on the underside of the shoots, are yellow, while the upright female clusters are red or yellow. The egg-shaped cones have upward-pointing scales and ripen in the first autumn after flowering.

OVAL *red young cones with upright scales are clearly visible on the slender, drooping branches, interspersed with needle-like leaves in clusters.*

conical habit

thin, drooping branches

NOTE

It is the deciduous leaves, upright cone scales, and yellow shoots that distinguish this species from the other larches.

female flower cluster

male flower cluster

cone to 4cm long

HEIGHT *30–40m.* **SPREAD** *15m.*
BARK *Grey and smooth; becoming red-brown and cracking into scaly plates with age.*
FLOWERING TIME *Spring.*
OCCURRENCE *Mountain forests in C. Europe; commonly planted for timber elsewhere.*
SIMILAR SPECIES *Japanese Larch (p.30), which has cones with the scales curved outwards.*

Japanese Larch

Larix kaempferi (Pinaceae)

CONE *scales curve backwards, making the cones look like rosettes.*

cone to 3cm long

leaf to 4cm long

male flowers

female flowers

This deciduous tree is characterized by slender and soft, blue- to grey-green leaves that open in early spring, turning yellow in autumn. They are arranged singly on long shoots, but are borne in dense whorls on short side shoots. Male flower clusters are yellow, borne on the undersides of the shoots, while upright, creamy to pink female flowers are borne in larger clusters on top of the shoots.

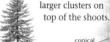

conical habit

HEIGHT *30m.* **SPREAD** *15m.*
BARK *Red-brown, cracking into scaly plates with age.*
FLOWERING TIME *Spring.*
OCCURRENCE *Cultivated (particularly for timber); native to Japan.*
SIMILAR SPECIES *European Larch (p.29) has upright cone scales and bright green leaves.*

Dunkeld Larch

Larix x marschlinsii (Pinaceae)

UPRIGHT, *egg-shaped cones have scales curved slightly outwards.*

green to grey-green foliage

This deciduous tree is a hybrid between the European Larch (p.29) and Japanese Larch (above), hence its alternative common name Hybrid Larch. Its slender, soft grey-green to green leaves, which turn yellow in autumn, are arranged singly on long shoots, but are borne in dense whorls on short side shoots. Male flowers are drooping and yellow, while the upright female flowers are cream to pink or red.

cone to 3cm long

conical habit

leaves in dense whorls

female flower cluster

HEIGHT *30m.* **SPREAD** *15m.*
BARK *Red-brown, growing scaly with age.*
FLOWERING TIME *Spring.*
OCCURRENCE *Cultivated; often occurs when seed is collected from Japanese Larch (above) growing near European Larch (p.29).*
SIMILAR SPECIES *None – it is intermediate between its parent species.*

Norway Spruce

Picea abies (Pinaceae)

A vigorous, upright evergreen, the Norway Spruce grows
very large and has many cultivars and varieties. Its slender,
four-sided, dark green leaves, with pointed tips, are
arranged on stout orange-brown shoots. Flowers
of both sexes bloom separately on the same tree.
The male flower clusters are upright, reddish
at first becoming yellow when ripe and
releasing pollen; the female flower clusters
are also upright and red, developing into
pendulous green cones that turn brown
when ripe.

CYLINDRICAL, *hanging
brown cones have
scales that are notched
at the tips, and fall
intact from the tree
when ripe.*

conical tip

leaf to
2cm long

cone to
15cm
long

female
flowers

male
flowers

large,
upright
tree

NOTE

The Norway Spruce
is the common
spruce of Europe
and frequently used
as a Christmas tree.
Many garden
selections are
grown, particularly
dwarf forms.

HEIGHT *50m.*
SPREAD *15m.*
BARK *Purple, developing scaly plates when mature.*
FLOWERING TIME *Late spring.*
OCCURRENCE *Forests, from Scandinavia to the Alps and Greece; on
mountains in the south of its range. Widely planted for timber and as an
ornamental species in gardens.*
SIMILAR SPECIES *Serbian Spruce (p.32), which has smaller cones.*

Serbian Spruce

Picea omorika (Pinaceae)

FLATTENED *leaves lie mostly above the hairy, pale brown shoots but some are all around.*

Conical when young, the evergreen Serbian Spruce eventually becomes narrow and columnar, with pendulous shoots. Slender, flattened, and needle-like, the leaves are glossy, dark green above with two white bands beneath. Male and female flowers are borne in separate clusters; the male flowers are red at first, yellow when open and releasing pollen; the females are red and ripen the same year to form pendulous, narrowly egg-shaped, purple-brown cones, to 6cm long, that fall intact from the tree when ripe.

P. omorika 'Pendula' is a garden selection with conspicuously drooping shoots that can spread across the ground at the base of the tree.

conical to columnar habit

leaf to 2cm long

two white bands on leaf underside

HEIGHT *30m.*
SPREAD *10m.*
BARK *Purple-brown, cracking into scaly plates with age.*
FLOWERING TIME *Late spring.*
OCCURRENCE *Native only to limestone mountain slopes near the River Drina in Serbia; commonly planted elsewhere.*
SIMILAR SPECIES *Sitka Spruce (p.34), which lacks the downswept branches.*

NOTE

This species is found very rarely in the wild and is now being threatened by hybridization with the planted Norway Spruce (p.31).

Oriental Spruce

Picea orientalis (Pinaceae)

An evergreen tree of dense habit, the Oriental Spruce is conical at first, becoming columnar with age. The leaves point forward on hairy pale shoots. Male and female flower clusters are borne separately on the same tree. Male flowers are red at first, yellow when open; female flowers are red, ripening to a slender, pendulous cone. The cylindrical cone is purple at first, later brown and sticky with resin, and falls from the tree intact when ripe.

NEEDLE-LIKE, *very short and rigid leaves are glossy, dark green and have four sides which end in a blunt point.*

NOTE

Commonly planted in large gardens. 'Aurea' is a very striking form with bright yellow young foliage.

leaf to 8mm long

cone to 10cm long

narrowly conical habit

HEIGHT *40m or more.*
SPREAD *10m.*
BARK *Pinkish brown, eventually flaking into small plates as the tree ages.*
FLOWERING TIME *Late spring.*
OCCURRENCE *Cultivated; native to the Caucasus and N.E. Turkey.*
SIMILAR SPECIES *None – the very short leaves and narrow cones of this spruce make it distinctive.*

Blue Spruce

Picea pungens (Pinaceae)

Narrow and conical when young, this dense, evergreen tree becomes columnar with age. Its four-sided leaves are rigid and sharp-pointed, ranging in colour from grey-green to bright silvery blue, particularly when young. Male flowers are red turning yellow; females are green, in separate clusters. Mature cones fall from the tree intact.

PENDULOUS, *elongated green cones are covered with tooth-tipped scales and ripen to brown.*

leaf to 3cm long

cone to 10cm long

narrowly conical habit

HEIGHT	25m.
SPREAD	7m.
BARK	Purple-grey, scaly.
FLOWERING TIME	Late spring.
OCCURRENCE	Cultivated; native to W. USA (Rocky Mountains).
SIMILAR SPECIES	None – the blue foliage and sharp leaves are distinctive.

Sitka Spruce

Picea sitchensis (Pinaceae)

Vigorous and large, this evergreen tree with a conical habit has smooth shoots that are white to pale brown. Its slender, glossy, dark green leaves are flattened, with a pointed tip and two white bands beneath. The clusters of male flowers are red, while the female clusters are green, maturing into pendulous, pale brown cones.

CYLINDRICAL, *hanging, and pale brown, the mature cones fall from the tree intact.*

cone to 10cm long

conical habit

leaf to 3cm long

HEIGHT	50m.
SPREAD	15m.
BARK	Purple-grey, flaking in large plates.
FLOWERING TIME	Late spring.
OCCURRENCE	Cultivated (particularly as a forestry tree); native to W. North America.
SIMILAR SPECIES	None – no other common spruce has flattened, pointed leaves.

Calabrian Pine

Pinus brutia (Pinaceae)

A conical to columnar, evergreen tree, the Calabrian Pine has slender, pointed, dark green leaves in pairs. The yellow flowers are in clusters, the males at the base of the shoots, females towards the tips. Borne on short stalks and pointing forwards along the shoots, the glossy brown cones ripen in the second autumn and fall from the tree intact.

MATURE *trees can reach a large size in their native habitat.*

rounded crown

leaf to 15cm long

cone to 11cm long

HEIGHT *20m.* **SPREAD** *10m.*
BARK *Orange-brown, cracking with age.*
FLOWERING TIME *Late spring to early summer.*
OCCURRENCE *E. Mediterranean region from Bulgaria to Greece and Turkey.*
SIMILAR SPECIES *Aleppo Pine (p.37), is more widespread and has bright green foliage.*

Canary Island Pine

Pinus canariensis (Pinaceae)

This evergreen tree is conical at first later becoming columnar. It has slender, dark green leaves with rough margins, borne in clusters of three. Young plants have bright silvery blue leaves, borne singly, and this foliage is sometimes retained for several years. Long-stalked cones, to 20cm long, ripen in the second autumn.

DISTINCTLY *conical when young, these pines grow on the volcanic mountain slopes of the Canary Islands.*

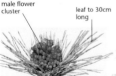

male flower cluster

leaf to 30cm long

columnar habit of mature tree

HEIGHT *30m.* **SPREAD** *15m.*
BARK *Orange-brown, thick.*
FLOWERING TIME *Late spring to early summer.*
OCCURRENCE *Cultivated (in plantations in the Mediterranean region); native to Canary Islands.*
SIMILAR SPECIES *None.*

Swiss Stone Pine

Pinus cembra (Pinaceae)

SLENDER, *pointed, and densely arranged in clusters of five, the leaves are bright green on the outer surface and blue-grey on the inner surfaces.*

Narrow and conical when young, this evergreen tree becomes columnar with age and has greenish shoots covered in orange-brown hairs. The slender, bright green, aromatic leaves are arranged in forward-pointing clusters of five on densely hairy shoots. The male flower clusters are purple-red, opening yellow when releasing pollen; females are red and in separate clusters. These mature to an egg-shaped, purple-brown, woody cone, up to 8cm long, which fall intact from the tree when ripe.

narrow, conical habit

leaf to 10cm long

HEIGHT *25m.*
SPREAD *10m.*
BARK *Grey-brown, scaly with age.*
FLOWERING TIME *Late spring.*
OCCURRENCE *Forests on mountain slopes, the Alps and Carpathians.*
SIMILAR SPECIES *Macedonian Pine (p.40), which has longer leaves, and larger, less woody cones. The closely related and similar P. sibrica grows over large areas of Siberia.*

NOTE

The cones do not open – the large seeds are either taken by birds or are released when the cone has fallen and decayed.

Beach Pine

Pinus contorta (Pinaceae)

The evergreen Beach Pine is usually bushy and
spreading when small, later becoming conical. The
short, twisted, dark green leaves are densely borne
in pairs on the shoots. Male flower clusters are
yellow; the red female flowers mature in the
second autumn into brown cones, up to 5cm
long. These often persist, open, for some time
on the tree.

EGG-SHAPED, *pale
brown cones point
backward along
the shoot; the
cone scales
end in a
sharp point.*

male flower
clusters

leaf to 5cm
long

young
green
cone

broadly
conical
habit

HEIGHT *25m.* **SPREAD** *10m.*
BARK *Red-brown, cracking into squares.*
FLOWERING TIME *Late spring.*
OCCURRENCE *Cultivated; native to
W. North America.*
SIMILAR SPECIES *Mountain Pine (p.38) has
dark brown cones); Lodgepole Pine (P.
contorta var. latifolia), has unopened cones.*

Aleppo Pine

Pinus halepensis (Pinaceae)

This evergreen, conical tree of open habit, spreads with
age. The very slender, bright green pine needles are
sparsely borne in pairs towards the ends of the shoots.
Male flower clusters are yellow, while the female flowers
are pink and mature to brown cones which
are borne in whorls of three on short,
stout stalks.

LARGE, *conical cones
point backwards along
the shoots and often
persist on the tree.*

open, spreading
habit

leaf to
12cm long

cone to
12cm
long

HEIGHT *20m.* **SPREAD** *10m.*
BARK *Grey, later red-brown and fissured.*
FLOWERING TIME *Late spring to
early summer.*
OCCURRENCE *Dry slopes in the
Mediterranean region.*
SIMILAR SPECIES *Calabrian Pine (p.35),
which has cones that point forwards.*

Bosnian Pine

Pinus heldreichii (Pinaceae)

THIS *species is characteristic of high mountain regions where it often grown on limestone.*

An evergreen, conical tree of dense habit, this pine becomes columnar with age. The rigid, dark green leaves are densely borne in pairs. While the male flower clusters are yellow, females are red-purple, maturing to egg-shaped cones that are deep blue in the first autumn, ripening to orange-brown in the next year.

leaf to 9cm long

red-purple female flower

conical habit

cone to 10cm long

male flower cluster

HEIGHT *20m.* **SPREAD** *10m.*
BARK *Grey and smooth when young; cracking with age.*
FLOWERING TIME *Early summer.*
OCCURRENCE *Mountain forests in limestone regions of S. Italy and the Balkans.*
SIMILAR SPECIES *None – its blue young cones are very distinctive.*

Mountain Pine

Pinus mugo subsp. *uncinata* (Pinaceae)

SMALL *and dark brown, the egg-shaped cones develop from female flowers, ripening in autumn.*

This is an evergreen tree of narrow, conical habit with needle-like, short, rigid, dark green leaves densely arranged in pairs on the shoots. The male flower clusters are yellow and female clusters are red-purple, maturing to small, dark brown, egg-shaped cones in the second autumn. *Pinus mugo* subsp. *mugo*, a shrub up to about 3m tall, is found from the Alps to the Balkans.

narrow, conical habit

cone to 5cm long

leaf to 6cm long

HEIGHT *25m.* **SPREAD** *10m.*
BARK *Grey-pink; black and scaly in old trees.*
FLOWERING TIME *Early summer.*
OCCURRENCE *Rocky mountain slopes from the Pyrenees to the Alps.*
SIMILAR SPECIES *None – the basal scales of the cone curve downwards making it easily recognizable.*

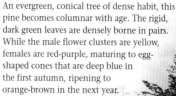

Austrian Pine

Pinus nigra (Pinaceae)

A stoutly branched, large, evergreen tree, the Austrian Pine is conical when young, becoming broadly columnar with age. It is often seen with several stems emerging from a trunk that is sometimes short. The rigid, dark green leaves have a sharp pointed tip and are borne in pairs. While male flower clusters are yellow, females are red, maturing to egg-shaped brown cones in the second autumn, that fall intact from the tree when ripe.

DENSE *stands of Austrian Pine can be found in the European mountains.*

cone to 8cm long

broadly columnar habit

leaf to 15cm long

HEIGHT *40m or more.* **SPREAD** *15m.*
BARK *Dark grey to nearly black, ridged.*
FLOWERING TIME *Early summer.*
OCCURRENCE *Rocky slopes in the mountains of C. Europe, from the Alps to the Balkans; also commonly cultivated.*
SIMILAR SPECIES *Corsican Pine (below), has slender, more flexible, grey-green leaves.*

Corsican Pine

Pinus nigra subsp. *laricio* (Pinaceae)

This large, evergreen tree is conical when young and later becomes broadly columnar, usually with a single trunk. The slender, flexible grey-green leaves are borne in pairs. Male flower clusters are yellow or red-tinged, while females are pink, maturing to egg-shaped, dark brown cones, up to 8cm long, in the second autumn. The cones fall intact from the tree when ripe.

conical to columnar habit

PINKISH *grey at first, the bark gradually darkens with age, developing ridges and scales.*

leaf to 18cm long

HEIGHT *40m and more.* **SPREAD** *15m.*
BARK *Pinkish grey; becomes dark grey, deeply ridged, and scaly with age.*
FLOWERING TIME *Early summer.*
OCCURRENCE *Rocky mountain slopes in Corsica and Italy (Calabria, Sicily).*
SIMILAR SPECIES *Austrian Pine (above), which has more rigid, shorter leaves.*

Macedonian Pine

Pinus peuce (Pinaceae)

GREEN *and resinous at first, the drooping cones later ripen to pale brown.*

An evergreen, narrowly conical tree of dense habit, the Macedonian Pine has slender, rigid blue-green leaves borne in clusters of five on the smooth green shoots. Male flower clusters are yellow or purple-tinged, while females are red. The female flowers mature in the second autumn to slightly curved, cylindrical to conical, pale brown cones.

conical, dense habit

leaf to 10cm long

cone to 15cm long

HEIGHT *30m.* **SPREAD** *10m.*
BARK *Grey-green and smooth; purple-brown and cracking into plates with age.*
FLOWERING TIME *Early summer.*
OCCURRENCE *Mountain slopes of the Balkan Peninsula (Bulgaria, Serbia, and N. Greece).*
SIMILAR SPECIES *Weymouth Pine (p.42) has narrower leaves and hairy shoots.*

Maritime Pine

Pinus pinaster (Pinaceae)

CONICAL *and glossy brown, the cone has sharp scales that end in a point.*

The evergreen Maritime Pine is conical when young, while old trees usually have a long, bare trunk and a domed head of branches. The very long, needle-like, grey-green leaves are rigid and end in a sharp point. They are borne in pairs, pointing forwards along the shoots. While the male flower clusters are yellow, females are red, maturing to prickly, glossy brown cones that may persist on the tree for many years.

conical habit when young

grey-green foliage

leaf to 20cm long

HEIGHT *30m or more.* **SPREAD** *10m.*
BARK *Grey when young, becoming red-brown and deeply fissured with age.*
FLOWERING TIME *Early summer.*
OCCURRENCE *Coastal regions and mountain slopes of S.W. Europe, from Portugal to Italy.*
SIMILAR SPECIES *None – it has the longest leaves of any native European pine.*

Umbrella Pine

Pinus pinea (Pinaceae)

This evergreen tree has an umbrella-shaped head of branches, unlike any other pine. Its grey-green leaves are needle-like, stout, rigid, deeply grooved on both sides, and and are borne in pairs on smooth orange-brown shoots. Young trees, and occasional shoots on old trees, have silvery blue leaves that are arranged singly. The flowers are borne in separate clusters on young shoots. While male flower clusters are yellow-brown, the female clusters are green, ripening in the third autumn to broadly egg-shaped to rounded cones.

GREEN *at first, the ripe cones are nearly rounded, heavy, and glossy brown. They contain large, edible seeds.*

broad, spreading habit

umbrella-shaped head

leaf to 15cm long

glossy brown cone

nut-like seeds

cone to 10cm long

HEIGHT *20m or more.*
SPREAD *20m.*
BARK *Orange-brown; deeply fissured on old trees.*
FLOWERING TIME *Early summer.*
OCCURRENCE *Coastal regions in sandy soils throughout the Mediterranean region.*
SIMILAR SPECIES *None – the flat-topped and spreading head is unique and makes this tree instantly recognizable.*

NOTE
The seeds of this species are the edible pine nuts or kernels that are commonly sold and often used in Mediterranean food.

Monterey Pine

Pinus radiata (Pinaceae)

UPRIGHT *male flower clusters are conspicuous on the tree in early summer.*

leaf to 15cm long

This fast-growing, evergreen tree is conical when young, later becoming broadly columnar. The slender, flexible, bright green leaves are densely arranged in clusters of three on smooth grey-green shoots. While the male flower clusters are yellow-brown, females are red, ripening in the second autumn to conical, pale brown cones that persist on the branches for many years.

broadly columnar habit

cone to 12cm long

HEIGHT *30m or more.* **SPREAD** *15m.*
BARK *Dark grey and deeply furrowed.*
FLOWERING TIME *Early summer.*
OCCURRENCE *Cultivated (for ornamental use and timber); native to USA (California).*
SIMILAR SPECIES *None – its bright green foliage, with leaves in threes, and persistent cones distinguish it from other pines.*

Weymouth Pine

Pinus strobus (Pinaceae)

RIPE, *pale brown cones are cylindrical, curved, and sticky with resin.*

The very slender leaves of this conical, evergreen tree are densely arranged in clusters of five on smooth shoots. They are grey-green on the outer surface and grey-white on the inner one. The male flowers are yellow, while females are pink, and are found in separate clusters on young shoots. The female clusters mature in the second autumn to pendulous, cylindrical, pale brown cones.

conical habit

leaf to 12cm long

bright yellow male flowers

cone to 15cm long

HEIGHT *30m.* **SPREAD** *15m.*
BARK *Dark grey and smooth; later fissured.*
FLOWERING TIME *Early summer.*
OCCURRENCE *Cultivated (sometimes for forestry); native to E. North America.*
SIMILAR SPECIES *None – although may be confused with less common Bhutan Pine (P. wallichiana) that has larger leaves and cones.*

Scots Pine

Pinus sylvestris (Pinaceae)

An evergreen tree, with branches that grow in whorls, the
Scots Pine is conical when young, developing a rounded,
spreading head on a tall trunk with age. The stout, needle-
like leaves are blue-green to blue-grey. Male flower clusters
are cylindrical and yellow, and found at the base of young
shoots. Female clusters are upright and red, and are
scattered in ones or twos at the tips of the young shoots.
They mature in the second autumn to
egg-shaped, woody green cones
that are brown when ripe.

YELLOW *male flowers nestle among the rigid and twisted blue-green leaves that are borne in pairs on the shoots; sometimes they have a silvery tinge.*

rounded,
spreading
head

orange to
pink bark on
upper trunk

NOTE

Many selections, particularly dwarf forms,
are cultivated in gardens. Of those that grow
into trees, P. sylvestris 'Aurea' has bright
yellow leaves in winter, while P. sylvestris
'Fastigiata' is narrowly columnar in habit.

HEIGHT *30m or more.* **SPREAD** *15m.*
BARK *Purple-grey, orange to pink towards top of trunk; deeply cracked,
and fissured, flaking into small plates with age.*
FLOWERING TIME *Early summer.*
OCCURRENCE *Heaths and mountains in sandy soils; throughout
Europe, extending east to Turkey.*
SIMILAR SPECIES *Distinct in the wild; may be confused with planted
Japanese Red Pine (P. densiflora) which has longer green leaves.*

female
flower

leaf to
7cm
long

male
flower

cone to
8cm long

Douglas Fir

Pseudotsuga menziesii (Pinaceae)

GREY- to purple-brown, the bark is thick, developing deep red-brown cracks with age.

A fast-growing, large, evergreen tree, the Douglas Fir is conical when young, taking on an irregular and flat-topped shape with age. Its slender, dark green leaves have two white bands beneath and are arranged radially, all around the shoots. Male flower clusters are yellow and found on the underside of the shoots. Clusters of female flowers are green or flushed with pink and borne at the ends of shoots. They later form long and pendulous cones with three-pronged bracts. Green at first, they become red-brown, and fall intact when ripe.

narrow-tipped branches

irregular habit

leaf to 3cm long

male flower cluster

female flower cluster

cone to 10cm long

HEIGHT *40m or more.*
SPREAD *15m.*
BARK *Grey-brown to purple-brown, deeply fissured with age.*
FLOWERING TIME *Late spring.*
OCCURRENCE *Cultivated (very commonly for forestry); native to W. North America, with a variety extending to Mexico.*
SIMILAR SPECIES *Blue Douglas Fir (Pseudotsuga menziesii var. glauca), which is smaller, has shorter cones, and blue-green foliage.*

NOTE

The three-pronged bracts on the cones make identification of Douglas Fir easy. The bracts, or their remains, can usually be found under the tree at any time of year.

Eastern Hemlock

Tsuga canadensis (Pinaceae)

The leading shoot at the top of this conical, evergreen tree is distinctly drooping. Arranged flatly on either side of the shoots, the leaves taper slightly from the base and have a blunt tip. On top of the shoot, the upturned dark green leaves point forwards, exposing their blue-green undersides with two white bands. Male flower clusters are yellow, while females are green, maturing to small, light brown cones.

PENDULOUS, *egg-shaped cones persist on the tree after shedding their seeds in autumn.*

leaf to 1.2cm long

drooping leading shoot

broadly conical habit

cone to 2cm long

> **HEIGHT** *30m.* **SPREAD** *15m.*
> **BARK** *Purple-grey, flaking in scaly patches.*
> **FLOWERING TIME** *Late spring.*
> **OCCURRENCE** *Cultivated (with many dwarf forms); native to E. North America.*
> **SIMILAR SPECIES** *Western Hemlock (below), which lacks the overturned leaves above the shoots and has parallel-sided leaves.*

Western Hemlock

Tsuga heterophylla (Pinaceae)

Like the Eastern Hemlock (above), this conical, evergreen tree is also characterized by a distinctly drooping leading shoot at the top. Spread on either side of the shoots, the dark green, blunt-tipped leaves have parallel sides and two white bands beneath. Both male and female flower clusters are reddish; males are borne beneath the shoots, while the females are borne at the shoot tips and mature into small cones.

narrowly conical habit

SMALL *and egg-shaped, the hanging cones mature from purplish red to pale brown.*

leaves to 2cm long

cone to 2.5cm long

> **HEIGHT** *30m.* **SPREAD** *15m.*
> **BARK** *Purple-brown, flaking and ridged as it matures.*
> **FLOWERING TIME** *Late spring.*
> **OCCURRENCE** *Cultivated (particularly for forestry); native to W. North America.*
> **SIMILAR SPECIES** *Eastern Hemlock (above), which has tapered leaves and smaller cones.*

Yew

Taxus baccata (Taxaceae)

ROUNDED, *pale yellow male flower clusters, about 3–4mm wide, are found in the leaf axils beneath the shoots.*

A broadly conical, evergreen tree, the Yew is often many-trunked. Linear and pointed at the tip, the leaves are dark green above, with two pale bands below, mainly spread in two rows on either side of the shoots. Male flowers grow beneath the shoots, while the tiny green female flowers are borne singly at the ends of the shoots on separate plants. The fruit is a single seed, held in a fleshy, usually red aril. It is open at the top, exposing the green seed, ripening the first autumn. All parts (except the arils) are poisonous.

'Fastigiata', or Irish Yew, is a selection with upright branches and leaves growing all around the shoots.

conical habit

upright branches

yellow aril

leaf to 3cm long

fleshy red aril with seed

'LUTEA'

NOTE

The Yew is often seen in gardens as hedges or topiary. Many selections have been made, including several with variegated foliage. 'Lutea' is an unusual form with yellow fruit.

HEIGHT *20m.*
SPREAD *10m.*
BARK *Purple-brown, smooth, and flaking.*
FLOWERING TIME *Early spring.*
OCCURRENCE *Hills and mountains, on chalk or limestone soil, throughout Europe; also cultivated.*
SIMILAR SPECIES *None – it is not easily confused with other species, especially when bearing fruit.*

Conifers with Scales

This group of evergreen conifers has tiny, scale-like leaves, and includes the cypresses and their relatives, as well as some, but not all, of the junipers. It is important to note that all conifers with scales have needle-like leaves during their juvenile phase as seedlings, only developing scale-like leaves as they mature. The Stinking Juniper (below) is a good example of this; the Chinese Juniper is less clear-cut, retaining some of its needles into maturity.

CHINESE
ARBOR-VITAE

LAWSON CYPRESS

WESTERN
RED CEDAR

PHOENICIAN
JUNIPER

Incense Cedar

Calocedrus decurrens (Cupressaceae)

DARK and glossy green, the leaves are in sets of two pairs, and have a triangular, sharp-pointed tip.

tapering towards top

A distinctly narrow and columnar habit, tapering towards the top, characterizes this evergreen tree. The aromatic, bright green foliage in flattened sprays is composed of tiny, scale-like leaves pressed against slender shoots. The flower clusters comprise tiny yellow males and green females, both borne at the tips of the shoots. The yellow cones, ripening to red-brown, are oblong with six scales that open out when ripe.

dense, narrow habit

cones open when mature

leaf to 3mm long

HEIGHT *30m.* **SPREAD** *5m.*
BARK *Smooth, red-brown, and later scaly.*
FLOWERING TIME *Spring.*
OCCURRENCE *Cultivated; native to western USA, extending south to Baja California.*
SIMILAR SPECIES *Some forms of Lawson Cypress (below), but the habit and foliage are different.*

Lawson Cypress

Chamaecyparis lawsoniana (Cupressaceae)

SMALL red male flower clusters are often conspicuous at the shoot tips in spring.

cone 8mm wide

The conical, evergreen Lawson Cypress has dark green foliage in drooping, flattened sprays. The tiny leaves are pointed, with white markings beneath and are densely arranged around the shoots. Male flowers are red; females are blue, ripening to rounded cones with eight scales, blue-green at first, later brown.

conical habit

densely arranged leaves

HEIGHT *30m or more.* **SPREAD** *10–15m.*
BARK *Purple-brown and smooth, later flaking in vertical strips.*
FLOWERING TIME *Early spring.*
OCCURRENCE *Cultivated (large number of forms); native to USA (Oregon and California).*
SIMILAR SPECIES *Western Red Cedar (p.57), has glossy foliage and egg-shaped cones.*

Hinoki Cypress

Chamaecyparis obtusa (Cupressaceae)

The dark green foliage of this conical, evergreen tree is arranged in flattened sprays. The tiny, scale-like leaves, which densely cover the shoots, have blunt tips and are marked with white beneath. While the male flower clusters are reddish yellow, female clusters are pale brown ripening to rounded cones – green at first, later turning brown.

RED-BROWN, *vertically fissured bark starts to flake in strips on older trees.*

narrow, conical habit

dense leaf cover

leaves with blunt tips

cone about 1cm wide

HEIGHT *20m.* **SPREAD** *8m.*
BARK *Red-brown, peeling in vertical strips.*
FLOWERING TIME *Spring.*
OCCURRENCE *Cultivated (many selections are grown in gardens, particularly dwarf forms); native to Japan.*
SIMILAR SPECIES *More common Lawson Cypress (left), which has pointed leaves.*

Sawara Cypress

Chamaecyparis pisifera (Cupressaceae)

A broadly conical, evergreen tree, the Sawara Cypress has glossy green foliage arranged in flattened sprays. The tiny, scale-like leaves have small, pointed, free tips and are marked with white beneath. Male flower clusters are brownish while females are green, ripening to small, rounded, brown cones that are green when young.

RED-BROWN *bark becomes fissured and starts peeling in vertical strips on old trees.*

leaves at angle to shoot

cone to 8mm wide

broadly conical habit

glossy green foliage

HEIGHT *20m.* **SPREAD** *8m.*
BARK *Red-brown, peeling in strips with age.*
FLOWERING TIME *Early spring.*
OCCURRENCE *Cultivated (many selections are grown in gardens, including forms with juvenile foliage); native to Japan.*
SIMILAR SPECIES *None – the small cones and free leaf tips make it distinctive.*

Leyland Cypress

x *Cupressocyparis leylandii* (Cupressaceae)

A very fast-growing, evergreen tree, the Leyland Cypress has a dense, narrow, columnar habit, tapering towards the top. The tiny, scale-like, dark green leaves have pointed tips. They are borne in small, flattened sprays densely arranged all around the shoots. While male flower clusters are yellow, females are green; both are clustered at the tips of the shoots. The glossy brown cones (which are not always produced on some forms) are green when young.

SPHERICAL *green young cones, when produced, ripen to brown the second year after flowering and so appear clustered on the old shoots.*

narrow, columnar habit

yellow male flowers

cone 2cm wide

densely arranged leaves

NOTE

This evergreen tree is a garden hybrid between the Monterey Cypress (p.52) and the Nootka Cypress (Chamaecyparis nootkatensis).

HEIGHT *30m or more.*
SPREAD *10m.*
BARK *Red-brown and smooth, ridged and flaking with age.*
FLOWERING TIME *Spring.*
OCCURRENCE *Known only in cultivation (several forms are grown, with various foliage colours, especially yellow).*
SIMILAR SPECIES *None – this species is quite distinct in its shape, vigour, and foliage.*

Smooth Arizona Cypress

Cupressus arizonica var. glabra (Cupressaceae)

This conical, evergreen tree of compact habit has slender, reddish shoots densely covered with irregular, aromatic sprays of tiny, scale-like, grey-green leaves. Each leaf has a pointed tip, and a small fleck of white resin is usually visible in the centre on the underside. The small but conspicuous male flower clusters are yellow while the females are green – both are borne at the shoot tips. Glossy brown, later grey, the rounded cones ripen in the second autumn.

REDDISH *purple to red-brown bark flakes in rounded scales as it ages.*

compact habit

dense leaf cover

cone 2.5cm wide

small flower clusters

HEIGHT *20m.* **SPREAD** *6m.*
BARK *Red-purple, flaky with age.*
FLOWERING TIME *Late winter.*
OCCURRENCE *Cultivated; native to USA (Arizona).*
SIMILAR SPECIES *Arizona Cypress (C. arizonica), is less frequently grown, has fibrous bark, and lacks resin on the leaves.*

Cedar of Goa

Cupressus lusitanica (Cupressaceae)

Also called the Mexican Cypress, this large, conical, evergreen tree has a rather open and sometimes weeping habit. Its foliage is dark grey-green, the tiny, scale-like leaves with free, pointed tips arranged in sprays all around the shoots. While male flower clusters are yellow-brown, females are blue-white and ripen in the second autumn to bloomy, rounded cones, with distinctly pointed tips to the scales.

VERTICAL *ridges develop on the bark as it peels in fibrous strips with age.*

grey-green leaves

open habit

cone 1.5cm wide

HEIGHT *30m.* **SPREAD** *10m.*
BARK *Brown, peeling in vertical strips.*
FLOWERING TIME *Early spring.*
OCCURRENCE *Cultivated; native to Mexico and Central America.*
SIMILAR SPECIES *None – the bloomy young cones with pointed scales make it easily recognizable.*

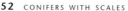

Monterey Cypress

Cupressus macrocarpa (Cupressaceae)

FOLIAGE *is arranged around the shoots as in all* Cupressus *species, and not in flattened sprays as in* Chamaecyparis *trees.*

A large, vigorous evergreen tree of usually dense, columnar habit, the Monterey Cypress spreads with age. Its aromatic, bright green foliage is composed of tiny, scale-like leaves with pointed tips, densely arranged in sprays all around the shoots. Male flower clusters are yellow, while females are green, both borne at the tips of the shoots. The rounded purple-brown cones have scales with small, blunt points. They ripen in the second autumn and usually remain on the tree for several years. Although a rare species in the wild, the Monterey Cypress is commonly cultivated in Europe.

bright green
foliage

dense,
columnar
habit

cone to
4cm wide

spray of leaves
around shoot

pointed
tips

NOTE

Several garden selections of the Monterey Cypress are frequently seen, particularly those with yellow foliage, such as 'Goldcrest'.

HEIGHT *30m.*
SPREAD *15m.*
BARK *Red-brown with shallow ridges.*
FLOWERING TIME *Early spring.*
OCCURRENCE *Cultivated; native to USA (coastal areas near Monterey, California).*
SIMILAR SPECIES *Italian Cypress (right), which has a narrowly columnar habit and egg-shaped cones.*

Italian Cypress

Cupressus sempervirens (Cupressaceae)

The narrow, columnar habit and tapered top make the evergreen Italian Cypress easily recognizable. Heavily fruiting branches may bend out from the tree under the weight of cones. The dark green foliage is composed of tiny, scale-like leaves with blunt tips, which are borne in irregular sprays all around the shoots. Male flower clusters are yellow-brown, while the females are green, both borne at the shoot tips. The egg-shaped to nearly rounded brown cones have 6–12 scales, each with a projection in the centre. They ripen in the second autumn.

CONES, *borne in clusters, are usually slightly longer than wide, with prominent projections on the large scales.*

tapered top

narrow, columnar habit

cone to 4cm wide

NOTE

The Italian Cypress is a characteristic tree of the Mediterranean region. Although the narrow form described here is most commonly seen, some are much broader and open with a conical or pendulous habit.

HEIGHT *20m.*
SPREAD *4m or more.*
BARK *Grey-brown with shallow, longitudinal, spiralled ridges.*
FLOWERING TIME *Early spring.*
OCCURRENCE *Rocky mountain slopes, S.E. Europe; also commonly cultivated.*
SIMILAR SPECIES *Monterey Cypress (left), which has a denser habit and smoother cones.*

Chinese Juniper

Juniperus chinensis (Cupressaceae)

LONG, *vertical strips peel off the bark, which is red-brown on mature trees.*

juvenile leaves to 8mm long

scale-like adult foliage

This conical, evergreen tree often bears two types of foliage. Juvenile plants have needle-like leaves in threes or sometimes in pairs, marked with two white bands above. Mature plants, on the other hand, have tiny, blunt-tipped, scale-like leaves, and usually some juvenile foliage. While male flower clusters are yellow, females are purple-green and borne on separate plants. The berry-like cones, 8mm long, are covered with a white bloom and ripen the second year.

conical habit

> **HEIGHT** *15m.* **SPREAD** *6m.*
> **BARK** *Red-brown, peeling in vertical strips.*
> **FLOWERING TIME** *Early spring.*
> **OCCURRENCE** *Cultivated; native to Myanmar, China, Korea, and Japan.*
> **SIMILAR SPECIES** *Pencil Cedar (p.56) also has both types of foliage on the same tree, but the cones ripen in one year.*

Stinking Juniper

Juniperus foetidissima (Cupressaceae)

RED-BROWN *in colour, the bark peels in long strips as the tree ages.*

The aromatic, dark green foliage of this dense, conical, evergreen tree is composed of tiny, scale-like leaves (needle-like in juvenile plants). Male flower clusters are yellow-brown, while the females, borne on separate plants, are green. These ripen in the second year to purple-black, rounded, berry-like cones up to 1cm wide, covered with a whitish bloom when young and bearing up to three seeds.

conical, dense habit

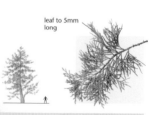

leaf to 5mm long

> **HEIGHT** *15m.* **SPREAD** *6m.*
> **BARK** *Red-brown, peeling in strips.*
> **FLOWERING TIME** *Early spring.*
> **OCCURRENCE** *Rocky mountain slopes in S.E. Europe and S.W. Asia.*
> **SIMILAR SPECIES** *Phoenicean Juniper (right), which has red-brown cones, foetid foliage, and a different distribution.*

Phoenicean Juniper

Juniperus phoenicea (Cupressaceae)

This evergreen tree is conical or sometimes shrubby, with dark green, slightly foetid foliage. While the leaves on adult plants are tiny and scale-like, on juvenile plants they are needle-like. Borne on separate plants, the male flower clusters are yellow and females are green. The rounded, berry-like cones are red-brown and sometimes slightly bloomy. They ripen in the second year and contain up to nine seeds.

TINY *scale-like, dark green leaves are arranged in pairs or in whorls of three.*

shrubby habit

HEIGHT *10m.* **SPREAD** *5m.*
BARK *Grey-brown, peeling in vertical strips.*
FLOWERING TIME *Early spring.*
OCCURRENCE *Coastal regions from Canary Islands and Portugal, throughout S. Europe.*
SIMILAR SPECIES *Stinking Juniper (left) and Spanish Juniper (below), which have cones in different colours and aromatic foliage.*

cones to 1.4cm wide

Spanish Juniper

Juniperus thurifera (Cupressaceae)

The aromatic, dark green foliage of this narrow, conical, evergreen tree is composed of tiny, scale-like leaves, often marked with a fleck of white resin. The plants may also bear juvenile foliage composed of needle-like leaves. Male flower clusters are yellow, while the female clusters are green, borne on separate trees. The rounded, purple, berry-like cones, to 8mm wide and each with up to four seeds, are bloomy when young and ripen in the second year.

conical habit

DARK *brown in appearance, the bark peels in vertical strips as it grows older.*

juvenile leaf to 5mm long

adult foliage

HEIGHT *12m.* **SPREAD** *15m.*
BARK *Dark brown, peeling in vertical strips.*
FLOWERING TIME *Early spring.*
OCCURRENCE *Dry hillsides in Spain and the Alps of S.E. France.*
SIMILAR SPECIES *Phoenicean Juniper (above), which has red cones, foetid foliage, and a coastal distribution.*

Pencil Cedar

Juniperus virginiana (Cupressaceae)

RED-BROWN *in colour, the bark peels off in vertical strips.*

This evergreen tree has a dense, conical to columnar habit. The aromatic foliage varies from green to blue-green and consists of both tiny, scale-like leaves and some juvenile leaves, which are needle-like and arranged in pairs. Male flower clusters are yellow, while females are green and borne on separate plants. The rounded, berry-like cones are blue-purple with a white bloom and ripen in the first year.

cone 2cm long

leaf to 6mm long

conical to columnar habit

HEIGHT *20m.*
SPREAD *4m.*
BARK *Red-brown, peeling in vertical strips.*
FLOWERING TIME *Early spring.*
OCCURRENCE *Cultivated; native to E. North America.*
SIMILAR SPECIES *Chinese Juniper (p.54), has cones that ripen in the second year.*

Chinese Arbor-vitae

Platycladus orientalis (Cupressaceae)

Usually rather shrubby with several main branches emerging from the base, this evergreen, conical tree has tiny, scale-like, dark green leaves. While the male flower clusters are yellow, the females are green and ripen to large, upright, egg-shaped brown cones, which are bloomy when young; each of the scales has a prominent hook on the back. These cones persist on the tree over winter.

TINY, *dark green leaves are arranged on the shoots in upright sprays.*

conical habit

cone to 2cm long

HEIGHT *15m.* SPREAD *5m.*
BARK *Red-brown, peeling in vertical strips.*
FLOWERING TIME *Early spring.*
OCCURRENCE *Cultivated; native to China, Korea, and E. Russia.*
SIMILAR SPECIES *Western Red Cedar (right), which has aromatic foliage and smaller cones.*

Western Red Cedar

Thuja plicata (Cupressaceae)

Fast-growing and conical, the evergreen Western Red Cedar has pleasantly aromatic foliage and its dark green leaves are borne in flattened sprays. While male flower clusters are blackish red, turning yellow when open, the females are yellow-green; both are borne at the ends of the shoots. The upright, egg-shaped cones ripen the same year from yellow-green to brown. Each cone has 10–12 leathery scales.

TINY, *scale-like leaves are dark green above, and have white markings beneath.*

narrowly conical habit

dark green leaves

cone to 1.2cm long

HEIGHT *35m or more.*
SPREAD *15m.*
BARK *Purple-brown, peeling in vertical strips.*
FLOWERING TIME *Early spring.*
OCCURRENCE *Cultivated; native to W. North America.*
SIMILAR SPECIES *Lawson Cypress (p.48), which has rounded cones with eight scales; Chinese Arbor-vitae (left), which has larger cones, and lacks the aromatic foliage.*

NOTE

A popular garden tree making an effective large screen. There are several selections including 'Zebrina' which have yellow-striped foliage.

Broadleaved Compound

A broadleaf tree with compound leaves has broad leaves (as opposed to needles or scales) that are made up of at least two leaflets. The leaflets may be arranged pinnately, and appear fern-like, such as on the Black Walnut, or they may be palmate and fan-like, as on the Horse Chestnut (below). Related tree species often have similar leaf types, but this is not always the case. For example, the Rowan has compound leaves, but the related Whitebeam does not.

STAG'S HORN SUMACH

JAPANESE ROWAN

PINK SIRIS

BLACK WALNUT

Paperbark Maple

Acer griseum (Aceraceae)

A deciduous species, this maple is broadly columnar at first, spreading with age. The leaves are divided into three leaflets edged with blunt teeth. They are dark green above, grey-blue and hairy beneath, and turn red in autumn. Small yellow-green flowers open in drooping clusters with the young leaves. They are followed by conspicuous fruit with broad, pale green wings that are usually seedless.

REDDISH *to pale cinnamon-brown, the bark peels in wafer-thin, papery flakes.*

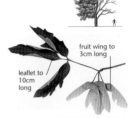

dark green foliage

leaflet to 10cm long

fruit wing to 3cm long

HEIGHT *15m.*
SPREAD *10m.*
BARK *Reddish to brown, peeling conspicuously in thin flakes.*
FLOWERING TIME *Late spring.*
OCCURRENCE *Cultivated; native to China.*
SIMILAR SPECIES *None – its peeling bark is unmistakable.*

Box Elder

Acer negundo (Aceraceae)

This deciduous tree, also known as the Ash-leaved Maple, has pinnate, opposite, dark green leaves, with 3–7 leaflets on smooth or hairy, often bloomy, shoots. Tiny, green to pink flowers, without petals, are borne in clusters before or as the leaves emerge, with males and females on separate plants; female plants bear two-winged fruit. Variegated, yellow-leaved forms such as 'Elegans', 'Flamingo', and 'Variegatum' are cultivated in gardens.

SMALL *clusters of downward-pointing, curved fruit are borne on female trees.*

leaf to 20cm long

'ELEGANS'

tassel-like male flowers

red anthers

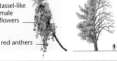

wide habit

HEIGHT *15m.*
SPREAD *10m.*
BARK *Grey-brown and smooth.*
FLOWERING TIME *Early spring.*
OCCURRENCE *Cultivated; native to North America.*
SIMILAR SPECIES *None – no other maple has leaves with more than three leaflets.*

Mastic Tree

Pistacia lentiscus (Anacardiaceae)

SMALL *and rounded, the fruit, 5mm wide, is red at first, ripening to black.*

Also known as the Lentisc, this small, evergreen tree of spreading habit is often shrubby. The alternate, leathery, dark green leaves are pinnate with up to six pairs of untoothed leaflets, which end in a small point, with no terminal leaflet. Each leaf stalk has a distinct wing. Small red or yellow flowers, without petals, appear in dense clusters in the axils of the leaves, males and females on separate plants.

spreading habit

leaflet to 3cm long

flower to 3cm long

HEIGHT *8m.* **SPREAD** *6m or less.*
BARK *Grey-brown.*
FLOWERING TIME *Spring.*
OCCURRENCE *Dry places, slopes, and woods in the Mediterranean region.*
SIMILAR SPECIES *Turpentine Tree (below), which is deciduous and has pinnate leaves with a terminal leaflet.*

Turpentine Tree

Pistacia terebinthus (Anacardiaceae)

RED *at first, the egg-shaped fruit, up to 7mm long, become purple-brown when ripe.*

Deciduous and spreading, the Turpentine Tree has alternate, pinnate, dark green leaves, with up to nine untoothed leaflets, each of which ends in a small, pointed tip. The small green flowers have no petals, and are borne in elongated clusters from the axils of the leaves, males and females on separate plants.

spreading habit

leaflet to 6cm long

flower cluster to 15cm long

HEIGHT *10m.* **SPREAD** *8m.*
BARK *Grey-brown.*
FLOWERING TIME *Spring.*
OCCURRENCE *Dry slopes and woods around the Mediterranean, from France to Turkey.*
SIMILAR SPECIES *Mastic Tree (above), which is evergreen and has leaves that lack a terminal leaflet.*

Stag's Horn Sumach

Rhus typhina (Anacardiaceae)

This deciduous, spreading tree of open habit, is often shrubby, producing numerous suckers from around the base. The alternate, pinnate leaves have up to 27 leaflets, which are dark green above and blue-green beneath, borne on stout, velvety shoots. Tiny green flowers are borne in dense, conical, upright clusters, on the same plant or on separate plants, followed by the fruit.

BRIGHT *red fruit are matted together with long hairs, forming conical clusters.*

broadly spreading habit

leaf to 60cm long

flower cluster to 20cm long

HEIGHT *10m.* **SPREAD** *10m.*
BARK *Dark brown, smooth.*
FLOWERING TIME *Summer.*
OCCURRENCE *Cultivated; native to E. North America.*
SIMILAR SPECIES *Smooth Sumach (Rhus glabra), which has smooth, bloomy shoots and minute hairs on the fruit.*

Pepper Tree

Schinus molle (Anacardiaceae)

The slender, pendulous shoots create a weeping effect in this broadly columnar to rounded, evergreen tree. The alternate, pinnate, dark green leaves have as many as 30 or more slender leaflets, which may be toothed, sometimes with a terminal leaflet. Tiny, creamy white flowers open in large, pendulous clusters in spring and summer, males and females are borne on separate plants.

ROUNDED, *aromatic, small, glossy red fruit, to 5mm wide, are borne on female trees.*

broadly columnar habit

pinnate leaf to 30cm long

HEIGHT *15m.* **SPREAD** *10m.*
BARK *Red-brown, flaking when mature.*
FLOWERING TIME *Spring and summer.*
OCCURRENCE *Cultivated (particularly in the Mediterranean region); naturalized in parts of S. Europe; native to Central and South America.*
SIMILAR SPECIES *None.*

Japanese Angelica Tree

Aralia elata (Araliaceae)

This deciduous tree or shrub of spreading habit has stout, spiny branches, and usually produces numerous suckers around the base. Opposite and twice pinnate, the leaves have numerous, dark green leaflets that turn yellow, red, or purple in autumn. The flowers are followed by tiny, rounded purple-black fruit, 5mm wide.

SMALL *white flower clusters, about 2.5cm wide, are borne at the end of shoots, the whole flowerhead up to 60cm long.*

spreading habit

leaf 1m or more long

HEIGHT *10m.*
SPREAD *10m.*
BARK *Grey and prickly.*
FLOWERING TIME *Autumn.*
OCCURRENCE *Cultivated (slow-growing variegated forms); native to E. Asia.*
SIMILAR SPECIES *Devil's Walking Stick (A. spinosa) has conical, upright flowerheads.*

Jacaranda

Jacaranda mimosifolia (Bignoniaceae)

A deciduous, spreading tree, the Jacaranda has opposite, fern-like leaves, which are twice pinnate with numerous small, bright green leaflets, to 1cm long; the leaf stalks are spiny beneath. Purple-blue flowers are arranged in broadly pyramid-shaped heads at the shoot tips, usually before the leaves.

DISC-SHAPED *seed pods, about 6cm wide, are dark brown and woody when ripe.*

leaf to 30cm long

flower to 3cm long

spreading habit

HEIGHT *15m.* **SPREAD** *10m.*
BARK *Dark brown with shallow ridges.*
FLOWERING TIME *Spring.*
OCCURRENCE *Cultivated; native to Argentina and Bolivia.*
SIMILAR SPECIES *Pink Siris (p.71), which has similar foliage but is not as large and has pink flowers with long pink stamens.*

Elder

Sambucus nigra (Caprifoliaceae)

With a broadly columnar to rounded head, a rather twisted growth, and arching branches, the deciduous Elder tree is often shrubby, with several stems sprouting from the base. The leaves, borne in opposite pairs on stout grey-brown shoots, are pinnate, with 5–7 sharply toothed, oval, elliptical, and pointed leaflets, each up to 20cm long; they have a rather unpleasant smell. The flat heads of white flowers, each about 6–10mm wide, are followed by glossy black, edible berries, which are green when unripe, and have red stalks.

SMALL, *creamy white, fragrant flowers are borne in broad, flattened heads up to 25cm wide.*

broadly columnar to rounded head

creamy white flowers

leaf to 30cm long

berry about 6mm wide

leaflet to 12cm long

NOTE

Both the flowers and fruit are used to make wine. Many selections are grown in gardens, including the purple-leaved, variegated, and cut-leaved forms. The ripe fruit are occasionally green.

HEIGHT *10m.*
SPREAD *8m.*
BARK *Grey-brown, deeply furrowed, and corky.*
FLOWERING TIME *Summer.*
OCCURRENCE *Moist woods and hedgerows all over Europe; commonly grown in gardens (and often escaped from cultivation).*
SIMILAR SPECIES *Danewort (S. ebulus), which is herbaceous; S. racemosa which is shrubby with red berries.*

Red Horse Chestnut

Aesculus x carnea (Hippocastanaceae)

This hybrid between the Horse Chestnut (right) and Red Buckeye (p.66) is a deciduous, broadly columnar to rounded tree. Its dark green leaves are opposite and palmately divided into 5–7 sharply toothed leaflets. The flowers emerge creamy white streaked with yellow, but later turn deep pink, blotched with red. They have five petals and are borne in conical, upright clusters. Rounded fruit contain up to three seeds ("conkers") and have few or no spines; they ripen from green to brown. 'Briotii', a garden selection that is occasionally seen, has deep red flowers and darker, glossier leaves.

REDDISH *pink flowers are a feature inherited from one of the Red Horse Chestnut's parent species, the much smaller Red Buckeye.*

columnar to rounded habit

deep pink to red flowers

finely toothed margin

leaf to 25cm long

flower clusters to 20cm long

fruit to 4cm wide

HEIGHT *20m.* **SPREAD** *15m.*
BARK *Red-brown, rather rough, and often develops burrs.*
FLOWERING TIME *Late spring.*
OCCURRENCE *Known only in cultivation (grown in parks, streets, and gardens).*
SIMILAR SPECIES *Horse Chestnut (right), which has whitish flowers and spiny fruit; Red Buckeye (p.66), which is a much smaller tree with flowers that have four petals.*

NOTE

In winter, the Red Horse Chestnut can be identified by its only slightly sticky buds, as opposed to the very sticky buds of the Horse Chestnut (right).

Horse Chestnut

Aesculus hippocastanum (Hippocastanaceae)

The familiar Horse Chestnut is characterized by the large, glossy brown and very sticky buds that appear in winter. Its flowers are white with a yellow blotch that turns red. They are borne in large, upright, conical clusters and are followed by distinctive green fruit that contain up to three glossy brown seeds or conkers. A deciduous tree with a broadly columnar to spreading habit, it has palmate, dark green leaves each with 5–7 large, sharply toothed leaflets with short stalks. The leaves turn orange-red in autumn. 'Baumannii', a selection of this species, has double flowers and no fruit.

LARGE, *creamy white flower clusters make a spectacular show in spring, in parks, streets, and gardens, where this tree is commonly planted.*

columnar to spreading shape

vigorous habit

leaf to 30cm long

flower cluster to 30cm long

HEIGHT *30m.*
SPREAD *20m.*
BARK *Red-brown to grey; flaking in scales on large trees.*
FLOWERING TIME *Late spring.*
OCCURRENCE *Mountain forests in N. Greece and Albania; commonly cultivated.*
SIMILAR SPECIES *Red Horse Chestnut (left), which has pink flowers blotched with red, and few or no spines on the fruit.*

NOTE

Although commonly planted in parks and large gardens, the origin of this tree was unknown for many years, until it was discovered in the wild in the mountains of N. Greece. The seeds are used in the game of conkers.

Indian Horse Chestnut

Aesculus indica (Hippocastanaceae)

The young, lance-shaped, bronze-coloured leaves of this deciduous tree are finely toothed and turn dark green with age. They are opposite and palmately compound, usually with 5–7 leaflets. The clustered white flowers have long stamens. The smooth, pear-shaped fruit contain up to three glossy brown seeds.

WHITE *flowers have a yellow blotch that turns red as the flower ages, and are borne in upright conical spikes.*

broadly columnar habit

flower cluster to 30cm long

leaflet to 25cm long

fruit to 7cm long

HEIGHT *20m.* **SPREAD** *15m.*
BARK *Grey and smooth.*
FLOWERING TIME *Early summer.*
OCCURRENCE *Cultivated; native to N.W. Himalaya.*
SIMILAR SPECIES *Horse Chestnut (p.65), which flowers earlier and whose flowers do not have protruding stamens.*

Red Buckeye

Aesculus pavia (Hippocastanaceae)

Five sharply toothed, glossy green leaflets, each with a short stalk, characterize the palmately compound, opposite leaves of this small, spreading, deciduous tree. The leaves turn red in autumn. The smooth, rounded to pear-shaped fruit each contain up to two glossy brown seeds and ripen from green to brown.

FOUR-PETALLED, *narrow red flowers are borne in upright clusters about 15cm long.*

broadly spreading habit

leaflet to 15cm long

flower to 4cm long

fruit to 5cm long

HEIGHT *5m.*
SPREAD *6m.*
BARK *Dark grey and smooth.*
FLOWERING TIME *Early summer.*
OCCURRENCE *Cultivated; native to S.E. USA.*
SIMILAR SPECIES *Red Horse Chestnut (p.64), which has larger, five-petalled flowers as well as larger leaves.*

Bitternut

Carya cordiformis (Juglandaceae)

This conical, deciduous tree becomes broadly columnar with age. Its opposite, pinnate, dark green leaves have 5–9 toothed leaflets. Yellow in bud, the small petalless flowers turn green – males in pendulous catkins to 8cm long in clusters of three at the base of the young shoots, females at the tip of the expanding shoots. The fruit is an inedible nut in a thin husk.

GREY *and smooth, the bark becomes thick, furrowed, ridged, and scaly with age.*

leaf to 30cm long

male catkin

broadly columnar habit

HEIGHT *20m.* **SPREAD** *20m.*
BARK *Grey and smooth when young; later ridged and scaly.*
FLOWERING TIME *Late spring.*
OCCURRENCE *Cultivated; native to E. North America.*
SIMILAR SPECIES *Other hickories, which do not have bright yellow winter buds.*

Shagbark Hickory

Carya ovata (Juglandaceae)

This broadly columnar, deciduous tree has opposite, deep yellow-green leaves with five to seven toothed leaflets. The flowers are small, green, and lack petals – males in pendulous catkins to 12cm long in clusters of three at the base of the young shoots, females at the tip of the expanding shoots. The fruit is an edible nut enclosed in a thick green husk.

CONSPICUOUS *green buds to 1cm long appear among the pinnate leaves, which have taper-pointed leaflets.*

golden yellow autumn colour

female flower

leaf to 40cm long

HEIGHT *25m.* **SPREAD** *15m.*
BARK *Grey-brown; peels in vertical flakes.*
FLOWERING TIME *Late spring to early summer.*
OCCURRENCE *Cultivated; native to E. North America.*
SIMILAR SPECIES *None – its peeling bark and leaves with five leaflets make it distinct.*

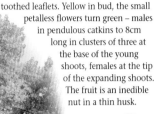

Japanese Walnut

Juglans ailantifolia (Juglandaceae)

GREY-BROWN *bark develops deep interlacing ridges on older trees, separating into small plates.*

A spreading, deciduous tree, the Japanese Walnut has stout, sticky shoots, densely hairy when young. The large, pinnate leaves have up to 19 toothed, dark green leaflets that are hairy on both sides. The flowers are small and without petals. The males are green, in hanging catkins up to 30cm long, on old shoots; female clusters are red, at the ends of young shoots. The fruit is an edible brown nut enclosed in a sticky green husk.

leaf to 90cm long

female flowers

broad crown

dark green foliage

fruit to 5cm long

HEIGHT 20m. **SPREAD** 20m.
BARK *Grey-brown, becoming fissured with age.*
FLOWERING TIME *Late spring to early summer.*
OCCURRENCE *Cultivated; native to Japan.*
SIMILAR SPECIES *Black Walnut (below), which does not have sticky, hairy shoots.*

Black Walnut

Juglans nigra (Juglandaceae)

SLENDER, *pointed, sharply toothed leaflets are glossy, dark green.*

This vigorous, deciduous tree is conical when young, but widens with age. The large, pinnate leaves have up to 23 leaflets, with the terminal one sometimes missing. The flowers are small and green, without petals; the males are in hanging catkins, and the females in small clusters at the ends of the young shoots. The fruit is an edible brown nut in a rounded green husk.

leaf to 60cm long

fruit to 5cm long

catkin to 10cm long

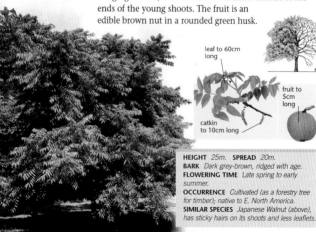

HEIGHT 25m. **SPREAD** 20m.
BARK *Dark grey-brown, ridged with age.*
FLOWERING TIME *Late spring to early summer.*
OCCURRENCE *Cultivated (as a forestry tree for timber); native to E. North America.*
SIMILAR SPECIES *Japanese Walnut (above), has sticky hairs on its shoots and less leaflets.*

Walnut

Juglans regia (Juglandaceae)

A deciduous tree, the Walnut has pinnate, dark green leaves with 5–9 leaflets, which are bronze when young. They are borne on stout, smooth shoots and are aromatic when crushed. The yellow-green flowers are small and without petals; males hang in conspicuous catkins up to 10cm long from the ends of old shoots, while the shorter female catkins form at the tips of new shoots as the leaves are expanding. The fruit is the familiar creamy white walnut, enclosed in a rounded green husk that ripens to brown. There are many garden selections grown for their fruit.

MALE *and female flowers are clustered in separate pendulous catkins on the same tree, the females shorter than the males.*

leaf to 45cm long

green husk

dark green leaves

broadly spreading habit

fruit to 5cm long

HEIGHT *25m.*
SPREAD *20m.*
BARK *Pale grey, smooth on young trees, becoming fissured with age.*
FLOWERING TIME *Late spring to early summer.*
OCCURRENCE *Mountains and hillside forests in S.E. Europe; widely cultivated for their ornamental value, fruit, and wood; often naturalized.*
SIMILAR SPECIES *None – no other walnut has leaves with so few, untoothed leaflets.*

NOTE

Walnuts can be distinguished from the related hickories (Carya) by the chambered pith, which can be seen if shoots are cut lengthways.

Wingnut

Pterocarya fraxinifolia (Juglandaceae)

A fast-growing, deciduous tree, the Wingnut usually produces suckers from the base. The large, pinnate leaves have numerous unstalked, glossy, dark green leaflets that turn yellow in autumn. The small, petalless, flowers are in hanging catkins, the males yellow and the females green. Small, green-winged nuts ripen to brown and are borne in long, slender, hanging clusters.

BARK *of mature Wingnut trees develops deep, interlacing ridges over the years.*

leaf to 60cm long

winged fruit in hanging catkin

spreading habit

HEIGHT *30m.* **SPREAD** *30m.*
BARK *Grey and smooth when young, becoming ridged with age.*
FLOWERING TIME *Late spring.*
OCCURRENCE *Cultivated; native to the Caucasus and N. Iran.*
SIMILAR SPECIES *Hybrid Wingnut (below), which has slightly winged leaf stalks.*

Hybrid Wingnut

Pterocarya x rehderiana (Juglandaceae)

A garden hybrid between Wingnut (above) and Chinese Wingnut (*P. stenoptera*), this is a vigorous tree with suckers at the base. The alternate, pinnate leaves have up to 19 toothed, unstalked leaflets and upright, winged stalks. The small, petalless flowers are borne in separate catkins, males yellow and females green. Borne in hanging clusters, the fruit is a small, green-winged nut that ripens to brown.

RIPENING *fruit clusters hang below the glossy, dark green foliage in summer.*

broadly spreading habit

leaf to 50cm long

fruit cluster

male catkin to 45cm long

HEIGHT *25m.* **SPREAD** *25m.*
BARK *Purple-brown, developing crossing ridges with age.*
FLOWERING TIME *Late spring.*
OCCURRENCE *Known only in cultivation.*
SIMILAR SPECIES *Wingnut (above) and Chinese Wingnut (P. stenoptera), lack an upright wing on the leaf stalk.*

Silver Wattle

Acacia dealbata (Leguminosae/Fabaceae)

An evergreen, broadly conical to spreading tree, Silver Wattle has alternate, bipinnate blue-green leaves divided into numerous tiny leaflets, each about 5mm long. Borne in large heads composed of many small, rounded clusters, the individual flowers are tiny. The fruit is a flattened pod, ripening from green to brown.

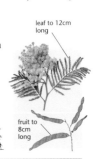

SMOOTH *and blue-green on young trees, the bark becomes nearly black with age.*

fragrant yellow flowers

leaf to 12cm long

fruit to 8cm long

HEIGHT 15m. **SPREAD** 10m.
BARK *Smooth and blue-green; becoming nearly black with age.*
FLOWERING TIME *Late winter to early spring.*
OCCURRENCE *Cultivated (Mediterranean region); native to S.E. Australia and Tasmania.*
SIMILAR SPECIES *Pink Siris (below), has dark green leaves and dark grey-brown bark.*

Pink Siris

Albizia julibrissin (Leguminosae/Fabaceae)

Also known as the Silk Tree, this deciduous tree has an open, spreading habit. The alternate, bipinnate, fern-like, dark green leaves have numerous small leaflets. Dense, fluffy clusters of flowers appear at the ends of the shoots. The fruit is a flattened pod, to 15cm long, that is brown when ripe.

SMALL *flowers in clusters are made conspicuous by long, silky pink stamens.*

broadly spreading habit

flower cluster

leaflets to 1cm long

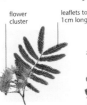

HEIGHT 12m.
SPREAD 12m.
BARK *Dark grey-brown and smooth.*
FLOWERING TIME *Late summer.*
OCCURRENCE *Cultivated; native to S.W. Asia and China.*
SIMILAR SPECIES *Silver Wattle (above), which has blue-green leaves and bark.*

Pea Tree

Caragana arborescens (Leguminosae/Fabaceae)

YELLOW *peaflowers up to 2cm in length are produced on slender stalks in small clusters.*

More often a large shrub, the deciduous Pea Tree is upright when young, spreading with age. The alternate, pinnate leaves, dark- to mid-green, have 4–6 pairs of untoothed leaflets, the terminal one being replaced by a bristle-like, slender spine. The flowers are borne on the previous year's woody growth and are followed by cylindrical brown pods up to 5cm in length.

shrubby growth

leaf to 8cm long

HEIGHT *6m.* **SPREAD** *4m.*
BARK *Grey-brown, smooth, and glossy.*
FLOWERING TIME *Late spring.*
OCCURRENCE *Cultivated in gardens and sometimes naturalized; native to N. Asia.*
SIMILAR SPECIES *C. arborescens 'Lorbergii' is a selection with very slender leaflets and smaller flowers.*

Carob

Ceratonia siliqua (Leguminosae/Fabaceae)

FLATTENED, *pod-like fruit, green when young, later turn purple-brown.*

An evergreen tree of broad, spreading habit, the Carob is also sometimes shrubby. Its alternate, leathery, glossy, dark- to mid-green leaves are composed of up to six pairs of untoothed leaflets and lack a terminal leaflet. Small green flowers are borne in cylindrical clusters, up to 15cm long, males and females usually on separate trees. The fruit, which does not split open, contains hard seeds in a sweet pulp.

spreading habit

leaflet to 6cm long

fruit to 20cm long

HEIGHT *10m.* **SPREAD** *12m.*
BARK *Dark brown and rough.*
FLOWERING TIME *Summer to autumn.*
OCCURRENCE *Dry, rocky areas and hillsides of the Mediterranean region; widely cultivated and naturalized in S. Europe.*
SIMILAR SPECIES *None – the foliage and fruit are very distinct.*

Honey Locust

Gleditsia triacanthos (Leguminosae/Fabaceae)

A deciduous tree with a columnar to spreading crown, the Honey Locust has a trunk that often bears large, branched spines. Alternate, pinnate or twice pinnate leaves made up of bright green leaflets turn yellow in autumn. The small flowers are yellow-green, males and females in separate cylindrical clusters about 5cm long. The fruit is a dark brown, often twisted, flattened pod up to 45cm long.

DARK *grey and scaly, the bark is rough and usually has clusters of branched spines.*

broadly spreading habit

leaflet to 4cm long

leaf to 20cm long

HEIGHT *30m.* **SPREAD** *20m.*
BARK *Dark grey, rough and scaly; sometimes spiny.*
FLOWERING TIME *Early summer.*
OCCURRENCE *Cultivated; native to E. North America.*
SIMILAR SPECIES *'Sunburst' and many other garden selections which are spineless.*

Alpine Laburnum

Laburnum alpinum (Leguminosae/Fabaceae)

Also known as the Scotch Laburnum, this small, spreading, deciduous tree, or shrub, has alternate leaves divided into three leaflets that are deep- to mid-green above, and glossy green, smooth, and slightly hairy below. The pea-like flowers, about 2cm long, are borne in hanging clusters that grow up to 45cm in length. The fruit is a pale brown pod, up to 8cm long, and is narrowly winged above.

FRAGRANT, *golden yellow flowers are borne in slender, pendulous clusters.*

pointed tip

spreading habit

3 leaflets

leaf to 10cm long

HEIGHT *6m or more.* **SPREAD** *5m.*
BARK *Dark grey and smooth; later fissured.*
FLOWERING TIME *Early summer.*
OCCURRENCE *Mountains of the Alps and Balkans.*
SIMILAR SPECIES *Common Laburnum (p.74), which has leaves that are silky and hairy beneath.*

Common Laburnum

Laburnum anagyroides (Leguminosae/Fabaceae)

PEA-LIKE, *fragrant, golden yellow flowers are borne in slender, pendulous clusters up to 25cm long.*

NOTE

All parts of this tree and of other Laburnums are poisonous.

Also known as the Golden Rain Tree, this deciduous, spreading tree has alternate leaves with three leaflets, each rounded at the tip. They are deep green above, grey-green and whitish beneath, and covered with silky white hairs when young. Golden yellow flowers are borne in dense and showy leafless clusters. The fruit is a slightly rounded, hairy, pale brown pod, up to 8cm long, with black seeds, and hangs in clusters. Although known as Common Laburnum, in gardens this species has largely been replaced by Voss's Laburnum (right).

broadly spreading habit

leaflet to 9cm long

flower to 2.5cm long

HEIGHT 7m. **SPREAD** 3m.
BARK Smooth and dark grey, fissured with age.
FLOWERING TIME Late spring to early summer.
OCCURRENCE Woods and thickets in mountainous areas of S. and C. Europe.
SIMILAR SPECIES Voss's Laburnum (right), which has slightly longer flower clusters and smaller fruit pods; Alpine Laburnum (p.73), which has leaves that are green and smooth beneath.

Voss's Laburnum

Laburnum x *watereri* (Leguminosae/Fabaceae)

The alternate leaves of this deciduous, spreading tree have three leaflets to 8cm long. They are deep green above with silky hairs pressed close to the leaf surface. Golden yellow, fragrant, and pea-like, the flowers hang in clusters 30cm or more long. The fruit is a brown pod, up to 6cm long, with few seeds, and is often sparsely produced. This tree is a hybrid between Alpine Laburnum (p.73) and Common Laburnum (left). 'Vossii' is the common form in gardens, with flower clusters up to 60cm long.

DARK *grey and smooth, the bark becomes shallowly fissured with age.*

flower to 2.5cm long

broadly spreading habit

HEIGHT *7m.*
SPREAD *3m.*
BARK *Smooth, dark grey; fissured with age.*
FLOWERING TIME *Late spring to early summer.*
OCCURRENCE *Mountains in S. Europe.*
SIMILAR SPECIES *Alpine Laburnum (p.73), Common Laburnum (left).*

Black Locust

Robinia pseudoacacia (Leguminosae/Fabaceae)

Often spreading widely by means of suckers, this is a vigorous, deciduous tree with a broadly columnar head. The alternate, pinnate leaves, on red-brown shoots, have up to 21 leaflets, usually with a pair of spines at the base. It has pea-like, fragrant white flowers in hanging clusters to 20cm long, and dark brown pods up to 10cm long.

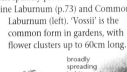

DARK *blue-green leaves have many elliptical untoothed leaflets, up to 5cm long, that are grey-green beneath.*

leaf to 30cm long

flower to 2cm long

columnar habit

HEIGHT *25m.* **SPREAD** *15m.*
BARK *Grey-brown with deep furrows.*
FLOWERING TIME *Early summer.*
OCCURRENCE *Cultivated, and widely naturalized; native to S.E. USA.*
SIMILAR SPECIES *Japanese Pagoda Tree (p.76) has green shoots without spines and produces smaller pods.*

Japanese Pagoda Tree

Sophora japonica (Leguminosae/Fabaceae)

FRAGRANT *flowers open in large clusters to 30cm long at the ends of the shoots.*

The smooth, spineless green shoots of this deciduous tree are bloomy when young and have alternate, pinnate leaves with up to 17 sharply pointed, untoothed leaflets dark green above, blue green below. The pea-like, white or pink-tinged flowers are about 1.5cm long. The fruit is a brown pod wavy-margined, up to 8cm long.

spreading habit

yellow autumn foliage

leaf to 25cm long

HEIGHT *20m.* **SPREAD** *20m.*
BARK *Dark grey-brown with prominent ridges.*
FLOWERING TIME *Summer; early autumn in regions with cool summers.*
OCCURRENCE *Cultivated and occasionally naturalized in Europe; native to China.*
SIMILAR SPECIES *Black Locust (p.75), which has angled, spiny red-brown shoots.*

Bead Tree

Melia azedarach (Meliaceae)

FRAGRANT *lilac flowers are profusely borne in large, open clusters.*

A deciduous tree of graceful, spreading habit, the Bead Tree has glossy, dark green leaves that are alternate and twice pinnate, divided into numerous toothed or lobed leaflets. Small lilac flowers, each with five spreading petals, are borne in clusters that are up to 20cm long. The rounded orange-yellow fruit, 1.5cm wide, often persist on the tree over winter.

spreading habit

leaf to 70cm long

HEIGHT *10m.* **SPREAD** *15m.*
BARK *Grey and furrowed.*
FLOWERING TIME *Late spring to early summer.*
OCCURRENCE *Cultivated (particularly in the Mediterranean region) and occasionally naturalized; native to S. Asia.*
SIMILAR SPECIES *None.*

White Ash

Fraxinus americana (Oleaceae)

This large, deciduous tree is of broadly columnar habit. In winter, its stout, smooth, green or brown shoots end in small, dark brown or nearly black leaf buds. The opposite, pinnate leaves have up to nine short-stalked and sparsely toothed, oval leaflets. Dark green above, they are blue-green beneath. The foliage turns to yellow, red, or purple in autumn, creating a spectacular sight. The tiny, petalless flowers of the White Ash are purple or green and borne in clusters, with males and females found on separate trees. The fruit, which are up to 5cm long, have a flattened wing, and ripen from green to brown.

GREY-BROWN, *the trunk develops narrow, interlacing ridges as it ages, unlike many other ash species, which have a smooth bark.*

bluish green foliage

broad, columnar habit

short-stalked leaflets

leaf to 35cm long

NOTE	
The White Ash provides a useful wood that is traditionally used in the making of sports equipment such as baseball bats.	**HEIGHT** *30m.* **SPREAD** *25m.* **BARK** *Grey-brown with narrow ridges.* **FLOWERING TIME** *Spring.* **OCCURRENCE** *Cultivated (with several selections grown for their habit and autumn colour); native to E. North America.* **SIMILAR SPECIES** *Green Ash (p.81), which has leaflets that are green below, not whitish.*

Narrow-leaved Ash

Fraxinus angustifolia (Oleaceae)

This deciduous, broadly columnar tree has shoots that end in brown buds. The opposite, pinnate leaves have up to 13 sharply toothed, taper-pointed leaflets, glossy bright green above, hairless beneath. Tiny, green or purple flowers without petals open in clusters before the leaves, males and females on separate plants. The winged fruit, up to 4cm long, are green ripening to brown. The leaves of the similar Caucasian Ash are often in threes, with slender leaflets that have hairs beneath near the base; a selection of this known as 'Raywood' is often grown for its elegant foliage and purple autumn colour.

GREY-BROWN, *the bark of the Narrow-leaved Ash has numerous, prominent ridges.*

broadly columnar habit

colourful autumn foliage

leaf to 25cm long

leaflet to 7.5cm long

NOTE

A widely distributed and variable species, the Narrow-leaved Ash is generally recognizable by its narrow and sharply-toothed leaflets.

HEIGHT *25m.*
SPREAD *20m.*
BARK *Dark grey-brown, with prominent ridges.*
FLOWERING TIME *Spring.*
OCCURRENCE *Woods and river banks of S. and E. Europe.*
SIMILAR SPECIES *Common Ash (right), which has distinct black buds; Caucasian Ash (F. angustifolia subsp. oxycarpa), which has different foliage and occurs from S.E. Europe to the Caucasus.*

Common Ash

Fraxinus excelsior (Oleaceae)

A large, deciduous tree of broadly columnar to spreading habit, the Common Ash has stout, smooth shoots and prominent black buds. The opposite, pinnate leaves have up to 13 sharply toothed, dark green leaflets, each 10cm long, with a slender, tapered point at the tip. Vigorous shoots from the base may be produced in summer and these often have purple foliage. The male and female flowers are separate, and may be on the same or different trees. Glossy green, winged fruit, produced in clusters, are up to 4cm long and ripen to brown.

TINY *and purple, the flowers have no petals; they are borne in dense clusters, and open from almost black buds before the leaves emerge.*

broadly columnar habit

leaf to 30cm long

fruit to 4cm long

HEIGHT *30m or more.*
SPREAD *20m.*
BARK *Smooth and pale grey when young, developing deep fissures with age.*
FLOWERING TIME *Spring.*
OCCURRENCE *Moist woods and river banks throughout most of Europe.*
SIMILAR SPECIES *Narrow-leaved Ash (left), which has brown buds and narrower leaves; Manna Ash (p.80), which has grey buds.*

NOTE

The distinctive flower buds form dense, nearly black clusters before they open and are easy to spot in early spring.

Manna Ash

Fraxinus ornus (Oleaceae)

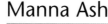

Also called Flowering Ash, this deciduous tree with a spreading habit has shoots with grey buds. The opposite, pinnate leaves, up to 25cm long, have up to nine dark green, taper-pointed, and sharp-toothed, stalked leaflets with hairs along the main vein beneath. They become tinged with purple and yellow in autumn. The fragrant flowers are followed by winged fruit to 4cm long.

FRAGRANT *flowers with four white petals are borne in drooping clusters to 20cm long with the leaves.*

broadly spreading habit

green fruit ripens to brown

leaflet to 12cm long

HEIGHT *20m.* **SPREAD** *20m.*
BARK *Smooth and dark grey.*
FLOWERING TIME *Late spring to early summer.*
OCCURRENCE *Woods on dry slopes in the Mediterranean region and E. Europe.*
SIMILAR SPECIES *Common Ash (p.79), which has black buds.*

Fraxinus pallisiae

Fraxinus pallisiae (Oleaceae)

The young shoots of this deciduous, broadly columnar tree are densely covered with soft white hairs. Pinnate and opposite or in whorls of three, the dark green leaves are up to 25cm long and have up to 13 toothed, slender-pointed leaflets that are densely hairy beneath. The tiny green flowers in clusters have no petals and open before the leaves. They are followed by winged fruit in autumn.

GREY-BROWN, *the bark is initially smooth, but gradually becomes fissured with age.*

columnar habit

leaflet to 6cm long

densely hairy shoot

HEIGHT *30m.*
SPREAD *20m.*
BARK *Grey-brown becoming fissured.*
FLOWERING TIME *Spring.*
OCCURRENCE *River banks in S.E. Europe.*
SIMILAR SPECIES *Narrow-leaved Ash (p.78), which does not have densely hairy shoots and leaves.*

Green Ash

Fraxinus pennsylvanica (Oleaceae)

A fast-growing, deciduous tree of broadly columnar habit, the Green Ash has shoots with blunt brown buds. Large, opposite, pinnate leaves have up to nine toothed or untoothed, distinctly stalked leaflets. They are glossy, dark green above, paler beneath, and turn yellow in autumn. The tiny, green or purple flowers have no petals and open only after the leaves. Male and female flowers are borne in clusters on separate plants. The winged fruit, up to 5cm long, ripen from green to brown.

GREY-BROWN, *the bark of the Green Ash has narrow, interlacing ridges.*

broadly columnar habit

leaflet to 12cm long

leaf to 30cm long

stalked leaflets

HEIGHT *20m.*
SPREAD *15m.*
BARK *Grey-brown with narrow ridges.*
FLOWERING TIME *Spring.*
OCCURRENCE *Cultivated; native to North America.*
SIMILAR SPECIES *White Ash (p.77) is often confused with this species, but differs in having pointed buds, and leaves that are blue-green beneath.*

NOTE

Two forms of this species were once recognized: Green Ash with smooth shoots, and Red Ash with downy shoots; they are now regarded as one species.

Canary Island Palm

Phoenix canariensis (Palmae/Arecaceae)

EGG-SHAPED, *dry-fleshed, orange fruit, up to 2.5cm long, are borne on female trees.*

This evergreen palm has a stout, single stem and a large, rounded head. The leaves, clustered at the end of an unbranched stem, are large and arching with up to 200 pairs of dark green, pointed leaflets to 50cm long, those towards the leaf base reduced to spines. Small creamy yellow flowers, 1–2cm long, are borne in large clusters which hang among the leaves. Male and female flowers are borne on separate trees. The Date Palm (*P. dactylifera*), which is taller, and is cultivated. *P. theophrasti* has blue green leaves and dry fruit. It makes a small tree to 10m tall with several slender stems and is only found in coastal areas of Crete.

large, arching leaves

leaf to 6m long

old leaf bases marked on bark

NOTE

One of the most commonly grown palms, Canary Island Palm is distinguished by its very stout trunk and long, arching leaves.

HEIGHT *20m.*
SPREAD *10m.*
BARK *Grey and rough, prominently marked by old leaf bases.*
FLOWERING TIME *Summer.*
OCCURRENCE *Valleys in the Canary Islands; commonly cultivated in the Mediterranean region and other warm areas.*
SIMILAR SPECIES *Date Palm (P. dactylifera) is larger, to 30m, often with suckers from the base, and has larger, succulent fruit to 7cm long.*

Windmill Palm

Trachycarpus fortunei (Palmae/Arecaceae)

Also known as Chusan Palm, this evergreen palm has a single, slender trunk and a small head of clustered leaves. The leaves are cut almost to the base into many, rigid, dark green segments, on a stalk to 45cm long. Small, creamy yellow flowers open in large clusters, males and females on separate plants. The fruit contains a single seed.

GREY *bark is mostly obscured by old leaf bases densely covered in brown fibres.*

fan-shaped leaf

leaf to 1m wide

male flowers

HEIGHT *10m.* **SPREAD** *3m.*
BARK *Grey and ridged.*
FLOWERING TIME *Late spring to early summer.*
OCCURRENCE *Cultivated in Europe; native to China.*
SIMILAR SPECIES *Petticoat Palm (below), which is larger and lacks the fibrous trunk.*

Petticoat Palm

Washingtonia filifera (Palmae/Arecaceae)

The stout, single trunk of the evergreen Petticoat Palm ends in a rounded to hemispherical, open head. The lower, dead leaves are long-persistent and hang against the trunk. The leaves, on a stout, spiny stalk to 2m long, are divided more than half way to the base into numerous segments. Small creamy white flowers are borne in large, hanging clusters to 4m long followed by egg-shaped brown fruit.

LARGE, *fan-shaped, grey-green leaves to 2m wide, are divided into about 50 segments.*

ridged bark

dead leaves

fruit to 1m long

HEIGHT *10m.* **SPREAD** *3m.*
BARK *Grey, ridged, mostly obscured by old leaf bases.*
FLOWERING TIME *Late spring to early summer.*
OCCURRENCE *Cultivated; native to China.*
SIMILAR SPECIES *Windmill Palm (above), is smaller with fibrous leaf bases on the trunk.*

Rowan

Sorbus aucuparia (Rosaceae)

Spreading with age, this deciduous, conical tree has shoots that end in purple buds covered in grey hairs. Alternate, pinnate leaves have up to 15 sharply toothed, taper-pointed, dark green leaflets, which are blue-green beneath. The small white flowers, each with five petals and conspicuous stamens, open in broad heads and develop into berries, which are poisonous when raw.

HEAVY *clusters of rounded orange-red berries, attractive to birds, often weigh down the branches.*

flowerhead to 15cm wide

broadly conical habit

leaf to 20cm long

fruit to 8mm wide

HEIGHT *15m.* **SPREAD** *10m.*
BARK *Glossy grey and smooth, becoming ridged with age.*
FLOWERING TIME *Late spring.*
OCCURRENCE *Woodland, mountains, and heaths on acid soils across most of Europe.*
SIMILAR SPECIES *Japanese Rowan (below), Service Tree (right).*

Japanese Rowan

Sorbus commixta (Rosaceae)

Broadly conical when young and spreading with age, this deciduous tree has shoots ending in sticky, glossy red buds. The alternate, pinnate leaves have up to 15 finely toothed, pointed leaflets, glossy green above and blue-green below, turning red and purple in autumn. Flat heads of small white flowers are followed by orange-red fruit in autumn.

ROUNDED *orange-red fruit, 8mm wide, are borne on red stalks.*

conical to spreading habit

leaf to 20cm long

flowerhead to 15cm wide

HEIGHT *10m.*
SPREAD *10m.*
BARK *Pale grey and smooth.*
FLOWERING TIME *Late spring.*
OCCURRENCE *Cultivated; native to Japan and Korea.*
SIMILAR SPECIES *Rowan (above), which has matt green leaves and buds with grey hairs.*

Service Tree

Sorbus domestica (Rosaceae)

The green shoots of this deciduous, broadly columnar to spreading tree end in sticky green buds. The alternate, pinnate yellow-green leaves have up to 21 oblong, toothed leaflets which are smooth above and hairy beneath when young, turning red or purple in autumn. Small white flowers, up to 1.5cm wide, each with five petals, are borne in rounded to conical clusters.

GREEN or flushed with red, the large, apple- or pear-shaped fruit have a gritty texture.

broadly columnar habit

leaf to 22cm long

flower cluster to 10cm wide

fruit to 3cm long

HEIGHT 20m.
SPREAD 15m.
BARK Dark brown, cracking into scales with age.
FLOWERING TIME Late spring.
OCCURRENCE Native to S. Europe; occasionally grown as an ornamental tree or for its fruit, and sometimes naturalized.
SIMILAR SPECIES Rowan (left), which has smoother bark, and smaller, orange-red fruit that are poisonous when raw.

NOTE

While mainly confined to the European mainland, this tree has also been found in South Wales. The relatively large apple- or pear-shaped fruit are sometimes eaten when slightly rotted.

Bastard Service Tree

Sorbus hybrida (Rosaceae)

This deciduous, broadly conical tree, becomes rounded with age. The alternate, oval, dark green leaves are covered with grey hairs beneath and normally have two pairs of free, toothed leaflets at the base, above which the lobes decrease in size towards the leaf tip. The flowers are in broad, flattened heads.

ROUNDED, *bright red fruit about 1.2cm wide follow the small white flowers.*

leaf to 10cm long

flowerhead to 10cm wide

rounded with age

HEIGHT *15m.* **SPREAD** *10m.*
BARK *Grey and smooth, cracking towards the base.*
FLOWERING TIME *Late spring.*
OCCURRENCE *Woodlands in Scandinavia.*
SIMILAR SPECIES *S. meinichii, has four or five pairs of free leaflets; S. x thuringiaca (right), has larger leaves.*

Sorbus teodorii

Sorbus teodorii (Rosaceae)

This deciduous shrub or tree has an oval head when young, later becoming conical to rounded. Its stout shoots end in purple buds covered in grey hairs. The alternate, pinnate leaves are dark green above with grey hairs below. They usually have four or five pairs of toothed leaflets, with a larger, three-lobed, pointed, and toothed terminal leaflet.

FLATTENED *white flowerheads, 10cm wide, are followed by rounded red berries.*

oval head

leaf to 10cm long

fruit 1cm wide

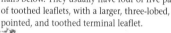

HEIGHT *12m.* **SPREAD** *8m.*
BARK *Grey-brown and smooth.*
FLOWERING TIME *Late spring.*
OCCURRENCE *Woods in Sweden.*
SIMILAR SPECIES *S. meinichii, which has leaves with a blunt-tipped terminal leaflet; Bastard Service Tree (above), which normally has two pairs of free leaflets.*

Sorbus x thuringiaca

Sorbus x thuringiaca (Rosaceae)

Deciduous with an oval to rounded head, this tree has alternate, narrow, oval leaves, usually with one or more pairs of free leaflets at the base. These are present on vigorous shoots but often absent on short, flowering shoots. The rest of the leaf is lobed, more shallowly towards the tip. The leaves are dark green above, grey and hairy beneath. Small white flowers are borne in flattened heads. 'Fastigiata' is a commonly grown selection, the upright branches making a dense, oval crown.

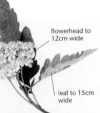

ROUNDED *bright red fruit up to 1cm wide are borne in arching clusters and make an attractive autumn feature.*

rounded head

flowerhead to 12cm wide

leaf to 15cm wide

HEIGHT *12m.*
SPREAD *10m.*
BARK *Grey and smooth, cracking with age.*
FLOWERING TIME *Late spring.*
OCCURRENCE *Woodland in Europe. A hybrid between Whitebeam (p.191) and Rowan (p.84) occasionally found where the parents grow together.*
SIMILAR SPECIES *Bastard Service Tree (left) has smaller leaves.*

NOTE

The compact, upright habit of 'Fastigiata' has made it a popular amenity tree, particularly where space is restricted.

Pride of India

Koelreuteria paniculata (Sapindaceae)

YELLOW, *four-petalled flowers, about 1.2cm wide, are borne in large, conical panicles at the ends of the shoots.*

The graceful shape of this deciduous tree, columnar with a broadly spreading head, makes it hard to mistake. The alternate leaves are pinnate, often with some leaflets further divided or lobed. Toothed and downy, they emerge bronze when young, turning dark green above, and finally yellow in autumn. Small yellow flowers are followed by bladder-like fruit capsules, up to 5cm long, yellow-green at first, becoming green or red, and eventually yellow-brown.

broadly spreading habit

flower clusters to 45cm long

leaf to 45cm long

3-sided fruit capsules

fruit to 5cm long

NOTE

There are a few garden selections. 'Fastigiata' is an uncommon form of narrowly upright habit. 'Rose Lantern' is generally grown for its red fruit pods.

HEIGHT 12m.
SPREAD 15m.
BARK *Pale brown with narrow fissures.*
FLOWERING TIME *Mid- to late summer.*
OCCURRENCE *Known only in cultivation; native to China and Korea.*
SIMILAR SPECIES *None – very distinct tree in all its features, particularly so in late summer and autumn when the characteristic flowers and fruit appear.*

Tree of Heaven

Ailanthus altissima (Simaroubaceae)

This fast-growing, large, deciduous tree has a broadly columnar crown. The alternate, pinnate, dark green leaves have 15 or more pairs of leaflets. Flowers are small, with five or six yellow-green petals and are borne in large panicles at the end of the shoots. Male and female flowers usually grow on separate trees, and the females are followed by winged fruit, up to 4cm long, similar to those of ash (*Fraxinus*). The fruit are green at first, becoming yellow-brown flushed with red.

PINNATE, *dark green leaves have many pairs of leaflets, which are tapered at the tip and untoothed except for 1–3 notches near the base.*

leaf to 60cm or longer

notch at leaflet base

columnar crown

dark green pinnate leaves

HEIGHT *20m or more.*
SPREAD *15m.*
BARK *Grey-brown with fine streaks, becoming darker and rougher with age.*
FLOWERING TIME *Late summer.*
OCCURRENCE *Cultivated; native to China.*
SIMILAR SPECIES *Walnut (Juglans) and ash (Fraxinus) species, which have opposite leaves without notches.*

NOTE

This vigorous tree thrives in warm cities where it is much planted, and often naturalized. In cooler areas, it may not flower or fruit well.

Broadleaved Simple

Most broadleaved trees have simple leaves – leaves that are not divided into leaflets. Both deciduous and evergreen trees fall into this group, and their leaf shapes range from slender to wide, untoothed to toothed or spiny, round to heart-shaped, and deeply lobed to shallowly lobed, such as the Red Oak (below). Technically, fan-leaved palms belong in this group but, in this book, they are included with the broad-leaf compound trees because of their superficial physical similarity.

NORWAY MAPLE

GREY ALDER

COMMON BEECH

BROAD-LEAVED LIME

Field Maple

Acer campestre (Aceraceae)

Also known as Hedge Maple, this round-crowned, deciduous tree of spreading habit is sometimes shrubby. The opposite leaves are dark green above, paler and hairy beneath, and turn yellow in autumn. They are heart-shaped at the base and deeply cut into five lobes, the larger of which have smaller lobes towards the tips. The leaf lobes are usually untoothed and end in fine points. When cut, the leaf stalk exudes a milky sap. Upright clusters of small green flowers open with the young leaves. The fruit is up to 2.5cm long, with two widely spreading wings, and hangs in clusters.

HANGING *in clusters, each fruit has two horizontal, spreading wings and ripens from green to reddish.*

round crown

spreading habit

leaf to 10cm wide

fruit about 5cm wide

NOTE

This species is often planted for hedging. Garden selections include forms with variegated foliage such as 'Carnival', with leaves edged creamy white and 'Pulverulentum', which has leaves speckled white.

HEIGHT *15m.*
SPREAD *10m.*
BARK *Pale brown, with orange fissures, and somewhat corky.*
FLOWERING TIME *Mid- to late spring.*
OCCURRENCE *Woods and hedgerows throughout Europe.*
SIMILAR SPECIES *Montpelier Maple (p.97), which usually has leaves that are three-lobed and lacks the milky sap in the leaf stalk.*

Snake-bark Maple

Acer capillipes (Aceraceae)

SMOOTH, *green and grey bark with vertical white stripes, on this and other maples has been likened to a snake's skin.*

The upright branches and young green shoots of this deciduous tree give it a broadly columnar to spreading crown. The opposite leaves have three taper-pointed, toothed lobes and are rich green above, smooth beneath. Small green flowers are borne in slender, drooping clusters, and followed by red-tinged fruit with spreading wings to 2cm long.

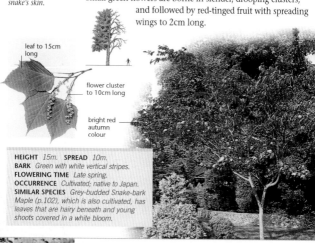

leaf to 15cm long

flower cluster to 10cm long

bright red autumn colour

HEIGHT *15m.* SPREAD *10m.*
BARK *Green with white vertical stripes.*
FLOWERING TIME *Late spring.*
OCCURRENCE *Cultivated; native to Japan.*
SIMILAR SPECIES *Grey-budded Snake-bark Maple (p.102), which is also cultivated, has leaves that are hairy beneath and young shoots covered in a white bloom.*

Cappadocian Maple

Acer cappadocicum (Aceraceae)

OPPOSITE, *bright green, leaves have 5–7 fine taper-pointed, untoothed lobes and turn yellow in autumn.*

This broadly columnar to spreading, deciduous tree, with green shoots, often produces suckers at its base. White sap exudes from the leaf stalks when they are cut. Small yellow-green flowers are borne in upright, rounded clusters with the young leaves and are followed by green fruit with spreading wings. Garden selections include 'Aureum' with yellow foliage, and 'Rubrum' with deep red young leaves.

columnar to spreading habit

fruit to 2cm long

leaf to 15cm across

HEIGHT *20m.* SPREAD *15m.*
BARK *Grey and smooth.*
FLOWERING TIME *Late spring.*
OCCURRENCE *Cultivated; native from Turkey to Iran and the Caucasus, with forms extending to the Himalayas and China.*
SIMILAR SPECIES *Lobel's Maple (p.96), which is upright in habit with bloomy shoots.*

Père David's Maple

Acer davidii (Aceraceae)

A small, deciduous tree of conical to widely spreading habit, this maple has opposite, glossy, dark green leaves. The leaves are oval, with a taper-pointed tip, and with or without small lobes at the base. They can turn yellow to orange or red in autumn. Slender, drooping clusters, 10cm long, of small green flowers appear with the young foliage. These are followed by green fruit that become flushed with red, then brown, and have spreading wings. Several forms are grown in gardens. 'Ernest Wilson' has pale green leaves turning bright orange in autumn. 'George Forrest' has large, dark green leaves with little autumn colour.

ONE *of the several mainly Asiatic trees known as snake-bark maples because of their attractive bark.*

conical habit

leaf to 15cm long

fruit wings to 3cm long

HEIGHT *15m.*
SPREAD *10m.*
BARK *Green with slender, vertical white stripes and marked with horizontal cracks.*
FLOWERING TIME *Late spring.*
OCCURRENCE *Cultivated; native to China.*
SIMILAR SPECIES *Grey-budded Snake-bark Maple (p.102) and Moosewood (p.99) both of which have lobed leaves.*

NOTE

This species is variable in its leaf shape and it is also one of the most commonly seen snake-bark maples.

Heldreich Maple

Acer heldreichii (Aceraceae)

With a broadly columnar to spreading crown, this deciduous tree has opposite leaves that are deeply cut, almost to the base, into three to five prominent, toothed lobes, the lower ones smallest. They are glossy, dark green above and blue-green beneath, turning yellow or red in autumn. The small yellow flowers are borne in upright, conical clusters as the leaves emerge and are followed by winged fruit. Red Bud Maple (*A. heldreichii* subsp. *trautvetteri*) from the Caucasus, is occasionally cultivated.

HANGING *in drooping clusters from slender stalks, the winged fruit ripen from green to red in the subspecies* trautvetteri.

columnar to spreading head

leaf to 20cm or more wide

yellow autumn leaf

reddish twig

NOTE

The Heldreich Maple is distinct from other maples in the very deeply cut leaves which may be divided almost to the base.

HEIGHT *20m.*
SPREAD *15m.*
BARK *Smooth and grey-brown, becoming fissured with age.*
FLOWERING TIME *Late spring.*
OCCURRENCE *Mountain woodlands in the Balkans.*
SIMILAR SPECIES *Sycamore (p.101), which has less deeply divided leaves and pendulous flower clusters; Red Bud Maple (A.h. subsp. trautvetteri), which has less deeply cut leaves and bright red fruit wings.*

Balkan Maple

Acer hyrcanum (Aceraceae)

Often shrubby, this deciduous, spreading tree has opposite leaves that are divided into sometimes three, usually five, lobes that are edged with few prominent teeth. They are dark green above and blue-green beneath and turn yellow in autumn. Small yellow-green flowers open in drooping clusters as the young leaves emerge, followed by fruit with two wings, which are green at first ripening to brown.

GREY-BROWN *and smooth, the bark becomes scaly with age.*

leaf to 10cm wide

shrubby to spreading habit

fruit wings to 3cm long

HEIGHT *10m.* **SPREAD** *10m.*
BARK *Grey-brown.*
FLOWERING TIME *Late spring.*
OCCURRENCE *Woods on dry mountain slopes in S.E. Europe.*
SIMILAR SPECIES *Field Maple (p.91) has smaller leaves; Spanish Maple (A. granatense) has smaller, hairy leaves.*

Fullmoon Maple

Acer japonicum (Aceraceae)

This is a deciduous, spreading tree, with rounded leaves that are silky and hairy on both sides when young. They have 7–11 pointed dark green lobes, which reach less than halfway to the base, and turn orange to red and purple in autumn. The small red-purple flowers are borne in hanging clusters as the young leaves emerge and are followed by fruit with two green or red-flushed wings. The large leaves of the garden selection 'Vitifolium' are richly coloured in autumn.

ROUNDED *and lobed, the opposite dark green leaves are edged with sharp teeth.*

spreading habit

HEIGHT *10m.*
SPREAD *10m.*
BARK *Smooth and grey-brown.*
FLOWERING TIME *Late spring.*
OCCURRENCE *Cultivated; native to Japan.*
SIMILAR SPECIES *Japanese Maple (p.98), which has leaves with fewer lobes and tufts of hair at the vein axils beneath.*

leaf to 13cm long

flower cluster

fruit wings to 2.5cm long

Lobel's Maple

Acer lobelii (Aceraceae)

SMOOTH *and pale grey, the bark of Lobel's Maple has shallow, vertical fissures, which appear on the surface as the tree ages.*

Deciduous with a narrowly columnar habit, this tree has young shoots which are covered in a blue-white bloom, becoming green the following year. The opposite leaves have five wavy-edged lobes which taper abruptly at the end to a fine point and have no or few teeth. They are glossy, dark green above, paler beneath, and turn yellow in autumn. A milky sap is exuded from the leaf stalk when cut.

Upright clusters of small yellow-green flowers open with the young leaves. These are followed by fruit with spreading green wings, which are up to 2.5cm long.

narrow columnar habit

yellow-green flowers

leaf to 15cm long

winged fruit

HEIGHT *20m.*
SPREAD *6m.*
BARK *Pale grey and smooth; developing narrow fissures with age.*
FLOWERING TIME *Late spring.*
OCCURRENCE *Mountain woodland in S. Italy.*
SIMILAR SPECIES *Cappadocian Maple (p.92), which has a spreading habit and does not have bloomy shoots; Norway Maple (p.100), which has several taper-pointed teeth on its leaf lobes.*

NOTE

This tree is very distinct in its habit, and is occasionally planted in gardens for its shape and autumn colour.

Montpelier Maple

Acer monspessulanum (Aceraceae)

Sometimes shrubby, this deciduous, spreading tree has a dense, rounded head. Leathery in texture, glossy, dark green above, and blue-green beneath, the small, opposite leaves are rounded at the tip with three untoothed lobes. Drooping clusters of small, slender-stalked, yellow-green flowers are followed by fruit with nearly parallel wings, up to 1.5cm long.

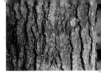

DARK *grey or blackish, the bark of this maple starts developing cracks in older trees.*

broadly spreading habit

leaf to 7cm long

HEIGHT *10m.* **SPREAD** *10m.*
BARK *Dark grey or blackish; cracks with age.*
FLOWERING TIME *Early summer.*
OCCURRENCE *Sunny slopes on hills and mountains in S. and C. Europe.*
SIMILAR SPECIES *Cretan Maple (p.104), which is evergreen; Field Maple (p.91), which has toothed leaf lobes.*

Italian Maple

Acer opalus (Aceraceae)

This deciduous tree has a broadly columnar crown. The opposite leaves are shallowly divided into three bluntly toothed lobes, sometimes with two smaller lobes at the base. They are glossy, dark green above, with few hairs beneath except on the veins when mature, and yellow in autumn. Clusters of bright yellow flowers open before the leaves.

Subsp. *obtusatum* has leaves that are hairy beneath, with shallow, rounded lobes.

WINGED *fruit follow the flowers; up to 4cm long, they are formed in pairs, in branched clusters.*

spreading habit

leaf to 10cm long and wide

bright yellow flowers

HEIGHT *20m.* **SPREAD** *15m.*
BARK *Grey-tinged pink, peeling in large, square plates.*
FLOWERING TIME *Early spring.*
OCCURRENCE *Woodland on hills and mountains in S.W. Europe.*
SIMILAR SPECIES *Sycamore (p.101), which has more deeply lobed and toothed leaves.*

Japanese Maple

Acer palmatum (Aceraceae)

BRIGHT *green above, the leaves turn yellow, orange, or red in autumn. The autumn colour is further enhanced by the green or red winged fruit.*

A deciduous tree with a graceful, spreading habit, this maple has slender shoots that end in small, paired buds. Borne in opposite pairs, the leaves are divided into 5–7 tapering, pointed, and toothed lobes, and have tufts of hair in the vein axils beneath. The small red-purple and white flowers open in clusters with the young leaves, followed by fruit with green or red wings, to 2cm long. Among the many selections grown in gardens are 'Atropurpureum', with purple foliage, 'Dissectum', a shrubby form with finely cut leaves, 'Osakazuki', with very good autumn colour, and 'Sango-kaku' ('Senkaki'), with bright pink winter shoots.

spreading habit

autumn leaf colour

leaves to 10cm long

tiny, red-purple and white flowers

HEIGHT *10m or more.*
SPREAD *10m.*
BARK *Grey-brown, smooth; slightly fissured on older trees.*
FLOWERING TIME *Late spring.*
OCCURRENCE *Cultivated; native to Japan, China, and Korea.*
SIMILAR SPECIES *Fullmoon Maple (p.95) has less deeply cut leaves with more numerous lobes, which, along with the shoots, are densely covered in silky hairs when young.*

Moosewood

Acer pensylvanicum (Aceraceae)

This is a deciduous tree with upright, arching branches and a broadly columnar habit. The opposite leaves are divided at the tip into three tapering, pointed, and toothed lobes. Deep green above and paler beneath, with some red-brown hairs, they turn butter-yellow in autumn. Pale green flowers in slender, drooping clusters are followed by fruit with green wings up to 2.5cm long. 'Erythrocladum', a form sometimes seen in gardens, has yellow bark, yellow-green leaves, and bright pink winter shoots.

GREEN with red-brown and white vertical stripes, the bark of the Moosewood becomes grey with age.

broadly columnar habit

NOTE
This species is one of the snake-bark maples, which are mainly native to E. Asia. The Moosewood (p.99) is the only one that occurs naturally in North America.

leaf to 15cm long

flower cluster to 12cm long

green fruit wings

HEIGHT *10m.*
SPREAD *8m.*
BARK *Green with vertical stripes.*
FLOWERING TIME *Late spring.*
OCCURRENCE *Cultivated; native to E. North America.*
SIMILAR SPECIES *Grey-budded Snake-bark Maple (p.102), which has bloomy young shoots, smaller leaves with coarsely-toothed lobes, and yellow-green flowers.*

Norway Maple

Acer platanoides (Aceraceae)

YELLOW *or red in autumn, the broad, bright green leaves each have five lobes, ending in several teeth with long, slender points.*

A large, vigorous, deciduous tree with a broadly columnar crown, the Norway Maple has shoots ending in red buds. The large, opposite leaves are divided into five lobes, each with several tapered teeth; bright green above, they are paler and glossy beneath, and turn yellow, orange, or red in autumn. The leaf stalk exudes a milky sap when cut. Clusters of small, bright yellow flowers open before the young leaves emerge, followed by fruit with large wings. Several forms are grown in gardens, such as 'Crimson King', with purple foliage, and 'Drummondii', which has leaves broadly edged creamy white.

autumn foliage

leaf to 18cm long

fruit to 5cm long

bright yellow flowers

NOTE
This tree is often confused in winter with the Sycamore (right). Both are common trees, but they are easily distinguished by the buds – red in the Norway Maple and green in the Sycamore.

HEIGHT *25m.* **SPREAD** *15m.*
BARK *Grey and smooth.*
FLOWERING TIME *Early spring.*
OCCURRENCE *Mountain woodland in Europe; commonly planted and sometimes naturalized.*
SIMILAR SPECIES *Lobel's Maple (p.96), which has bloomy shoots; Sugar Maple (p.103) lacks milky sap in the leaf stalk and has leaves that are blue-green beneath; Sycamore (right), which has green buds.*

Sycamore

Acer pseudoplatanus (Aceraceae)

The broad crown of this large, deciduous tree spreads with age. Its shoots end in green buds and the opposite leaves are divided into five sharp-toothed lobes. The leaves are dark green above and blue-grey beneath, turning yellow in autumn. Small yellow-green flowers are borne in dense, drooping panicles, followed by fruit with green or red-flushed wings. Several selections are grown in gardens, such as 'Atropurpureum', which has leaves with purple undersides, 'Brilliantissimum', a small tree with bright pink young foliage, and 'Erythrocarpum', which has red fruit wings.

YELLOW-GREEN *flowers hang in pendulous clusters from the slender shoots; the leaves are heart-shaped at the base and palmately lobed.*

dense foliage

broad, columnar head

leaf to 15cm wide

5-lobed leaf

flower cluster to 12cm long

fruit wing to 3cm long

'ERYTHROCARPUM'

NOTE

This species is known as a plane tree in Scotland but has no connection with the true planes (Platanus). The leaves are very often infected by tar spot fungus, which causes conspicuous black blotches.

HEIGHT *30m.* **SPREAD** *20m.*
BARK *Pinkish to yellow-grey, flaking in irregular plates when old.*
FLOWERING TIME *Mid-spring.*
OCCURRENCE *Mountain woodland of Europe; commonly planted and naturalized.*
SIMILAR SPECIES *Italian Maple (p.97), which has yellow flowers and bark which peels in square plates; Norway Maple (left), which has red buds.*

Red Maple

Acer rubrum (Aceraceae)

BRIGHT *red foliage in autumn gives the Red Maple its common name.*

The red to red-brown shoots of this large, deciduous tree have opposite leaves with three or five toothed lobes that reach halfway to the base of the leaf. Glossy, dark green above, they are blue-white beneath. Dense clusters of small red flowers, males and females sometimes on separate trees, open before the leaves, and are followed by red-winged fruit that appear on elongated stalks.

slender flower stalks

broadly columnar crown

leaf to 10cm long

HEIGHT *25m.* **SPREAD** *15m.*
BARK *Dark grey and smooth.*
FLOWERING TIME *Early spring.*
OCCURRENCE *Cultivated; native to E. North America.*
SIMILAR SPECIES *Silver Maple (right), which has larger, more deeply cut leaves, usually turning yellow in autumn.*

Grey-budded Snake-bark Maple

Acer rufinerve (Aceraceae)

VERTICAL *white stripes and diamond-shaped marks appear on the bark, which turns from green to grey with age.*

The young shoots and buds of this deciduous tree have a blue-white bloom. The opposite leaves have three prominent, toothed lobes; dark green above, they have red-brown hairs on the veins beneath. Small yellow-green flowers appear with the young leaves, followed by fruit with two green, red-flushed wings.

fruit to 2cm long

leaf to 13cm long

broadly columnar habit

yellow-green flower cluster

HEIGHT *10m.* **SPREAD** *8m.*
BARK *Green with long white stripes; grey and fissured on old trees.*
FLOWERING TIME *Mid-spring.*
OCCURRENCE *Cultivated; native to Japan.*
SIMILAR SPECIES *Moosewood (p.99), which has similarly shaped but larger leaves.*

Silver Maple

Acer saccharinum (Aceraceae)

Characteristic light green leaves with a silvery white underside lend this fast-growing, large, deciduous tree its name. The opposite leaves are divided into five deeply cut lobes, reaching more than halfway to the base of the leaf, and turn yellow in autumn. Small, yellow-green to reddish flowers open in clusters before the leaves, followed by two-winged fruit that are about 5cm long.

SILVERY WHITE *on the underside, the finely haired leaves are sharp-toothed.*

lobes reach below centre of leaf

columnar habit

leaf to 15cm long

HEIGHT *30m.* **SPREAD** *20m.*
BARK *Grey and smooth; flaking on old trees.*
FLOWERING TIME *Early spring.*
OCCURRENCE *Cultivated; native to E. North America.*
SIMILAR SPECIES *Red Maple (left), which has smaller, less deeply cut leaves that turn red in autumn.*

Sugar Maple

Acer saccharum (Aceraceae)

Maple syrup is made from the sap of this deciduous tree in its native North America. The opposite leaves have five lobes, the three larger ones bearing few round-tipped teeth. Deep matt green above, they are pale blue-green beneath, and turn yellow then to orange or red in autumn. Small yellow-green flowers open in pendulous clusters, followed by fruit with two wings, up to 2.5cm in length.

DEEP *fissures appear on the grey-brown bark with age; on younger trees it is smooth.*

broadly columnar habit

leaf to 13cm long

HEIGHT *25m.* **SPREAD** *15m.*
BARK *Grey-brown and smooth; fissured and scaly on old trees.*
FLOWERING TIME *Late spring.*
OCCURRENCE *Cultivated; native to E. North America.*
SIMILAR SPECIES *Norway Maple (p.100), whose leaves are green below.*

Cretan Maple

Acer sempervirens (Aceraceae)

CLUSTERS *of tiny winged fruit follow the small yellow-green flowers.*

This is an evergreen or nearly evergreen, spreading tree, often of shrubby, bushy habit. The opposite, short-stalked, leathery leaves are shallowly three-lobed or unlobed, often with wavy margins. Glossy, dark green above, they are paler below. Yellow-green flower clusters are followed by small fruit, which have two green or red-tinged wings up to 1.5cm long.

bushy habit

3-lobed leaf

leaf to 5cm long

HEIGHT *10m.* **SPREAD** *10m.*
BARK *Dark grey.*
FLOWERING TIME *Late spring.*
OCCURRENCE *Dry rocky slopes in the hills and mountains of Greece, including Crete.*
SIMILAR SPECIES *Montpelier Maple (p.97), which has leaves that are blue-green beneath.*

Tatarian Maple

Acer tataricum (Aceraceae)

SHARP-*toothed and oval, the leaves often turn orange or red in autumn.*

This bushy-headed, small, deciduous tree of spreading habit, is sometimes shrubby. The opposite, bright green leaves are unlobed or have a small lobe on each side. Small, upright clusters of white or greenish white flowers open after the leaves have emerged and are followed by fruit which are green when unripe, often turning red, then brown, with two green or red-tinged nearly parallel wings.

spreading habit

leaf to 10cm long

fruit wings to 2.5cm long

HEIGHT *10m.* **SPREAD** *10m.*
BARK *Grey-brown and smooth.*
FLOWERING TIME *Late spring.*
OCCURRENCE *Woodland and among shrubs in S.E. Europe and Turkey.*
SIMILAR SPECIES *None – it is very distinct from other* Acer *species, especially in its white, fragrant flowers.*

Highclere Holly

Ilex x *altaclerensis* (Aquifoliaceae)

YELLOW-*splashed, the leaves of the female form 'Lawsoniana' have a nearly spineless margin.*

An evergreen, broadly columnar to conical tree, the Highclere Holly has alternate, oblong to broadly oval leaves, that may or may not have spine-tipped teeth on the margins. They are glossy, dark green above, and variegated in some forms. Small, fragrant, white or purple-flushed flowers are borne in clusters, the male and female flowers on separate plants. Female trees bear bright red, rounded berries. Popular forms of this hybrid include 'Golden King', a female with yellow-margined leaves, 'Camelliifolia', a female with glossy dark green, nearly spineless leaves, and 'Hodginsii', a male tree with purple shoots and large leaves with fewer spines.

columnar to conical habit

leaf to 13cm long

'CAMELLIIFOLIA'

berry about 1cm wide

'GOLDEN KING'

NOTE

A hybrid between the various forms of holly and Madeira Holly (p.107), this tree was first raised in Britain when the latter was grown in glasshouses.

HEIGHT *15m.*
SPREAD *10m.*
BARK *Grey and smooth.*
FLOWERING TIME *Late spring.*
OCCURRENCE *Cultivated (in gardens); almost entirely represented by selections which are often variegated.*
SIMILAR SPECIES *Common Holly (p.106), which is found in the wild and has smaller, more spiny leaves, and smaller fruit.*

Common Holly

Ilex aquifolium (Aquifoliaceae)

This broadly columnar to conical, evergreen tree is sometimes shrubby, with green or purple shoots. Glossy and dark green, its alternate leaves vary in shape, from oval to oblong. Young trees and lower shoots tend to have very spiny leaves while on older trees and higher shoots, the leaves are smooth, so the same tree may carry both toothed and untoothed leaves. White or purple-flushed, fragrant flowers are borne in clusters, with males and females on separate trees.

SHINY, usually bright red berries are densely clustered on the branches of female trees. The 1cm-wide berries may also be yellow or orange.

columnar to conical habit

white male flowers

green ovary of female flower

leaf to 10cm long

NOTE

Many decorative forms exist in gardens, often with variegated foliage, such as 'Bacciflava', which bears yellow berries and has spiny leaves, and 'Handsworth New Silver' with red berries, purple shoots, and cream-edged leaves.

HEIGHT 20m. **SPREAD** 15m.
BARK Pale grey and smooth.
FLOWERING TIME Late spring.
OCCURRENCE Woods and hedgerows in Europe.
SIMILAR SPECIES Highclere Holly (p.105), which has larger leaves and fruit; Madeira Holly (right), which has winged leaf stalks and is found only in Madeira, although forms of it are found on the Azores and the Canary Islands.

Madeira Holly

Ilex perado (Aquifoliaceae)

This evergreen tree with a conical to broadly columnar head has alternate, dark green leaves that are borne on distinctly winged stalks. Clusters of small white flowers, males and females on separate plants, are followed by green berries that turn red. Subspecies *azorica* with smaller leaves is found in the Azores while subsp. *platyphylla* with larger leaves is found in the Canary Islands.

OVAL *leaves are untoothed or edged, with few, short, spiny teeth towards the tip. Female trees bear clusters of small berries, 1cm wide.*

crowded, glossy green leaves

leaf to 10cm long

HEIGHT *8m.*
SPREAD *6m.*
BARK *Grey and smooth.*
FLOWERING TIME *Late spring.*
OCCURRENCE *Woodlands in Madeira.*
SIMILAR SPECIES *Common Holly (left), which does not have winged leaf stalks but has spinier leaves on young trees.*

Italian Alder

Alnus cordata (Betulaceae)

A vigorous, deciduous tree, this alder is easily recognized by its distinctive rounded, alternate leaves that are finely toothed and heart-shaped at the base. They are glossy, dark green and smooth above, and paler with hairs in the vein axils beneath. The tiny flowers are borne in catkins before the leaves emerge, the males yellow and drooping, the females small, red, and upright.

WOODY, *brown, cone-like fruit can persist until the following year.*

conical habit

male catkin to 7.5cm long

leaf to 10cm long

fruit to 3cm long

HEIGHT *25m.* **SPREAD** *12m.*
BARK *Grey and smooth, developing shallow fissures with age.*
FLOWERING TIME *Late winter to early spring.*
OCCURRENCE *Woods in the mountains of C. and S. Italy and Corsica; frequently planted.*
SIMILAR SPECIES *None.*

Alder

Alnus glutinosa (Betulaceae)

SMALL *green unripe fruit are borne in clusters and mature to woody, dark brown cones that remain on the tree during winter.*

The Alder is a deciduous tree of conical habit, whose young green shoots and alternate leaves are slightly sticky to the touch. The dark green, mature leaves, paler beneath, are up to 10cm long; they are widest at the tip, which may be indented, and have a tapering base. The tiny flowers are borne in separate male and female catkins formed during the summer. The males are pendulous and yellow, to 10cm long; the upright, red females are much smaller, only about 5mm long.

conical habit

green unripe fruit

ripe fruit 2cm long

HEIGHT *25m.*
SPREAD *12m.*
BARK *Dark grey; cracks into square plates on old trees.*
FLOWERING TIME *Early spring.*
OCCURRENCE *River banks and other wet places in Europe.*
SIMILAR SPECIES *None – the leaves, broadest at the end with a notched tip, are distinct in shape from other European species of* Alnus.

Grey Alder

Alnus incana (Betulaceae)

This deciduous tree with a broadly conical habit has young shoots covered in grey hairs. Its alternate leaves are dark green. The tiny flowers are borne in catkins: the males drooping and yellow; the smaller females upright and red. The brown, woody, cone-like fruit, to 2cm long, may persist until the following year.

OVAL *and tapering to the base, the dark green leaves are grey and hairy below, and double-toothed or slightly lobed at the margins.*

broad, conical habit

HEIGHT *20m.* **SPREAD** *12m.*
BARK *Dark grey and smooth.*
FLOWERING TIME *Late winter to early spring.*
OCCURRENCE *River banks and other wet places in the mountains of Europe, east up to the Caucasus.*
SIMILAR SPECIES *Speckled Alder (below), which is a smaller tree.*

leaf to 10cm long

male catkin to 10cm long

Speckled Alder

Alnus rugosa (Betulaceae)

This sometimes shrubby, small, deciduous tree of spreading habit has slightly hairy young shoots. Its alternate, oval leaves are dark green and deeply veined above, greenish white beneath, and are edged with small, double teeth. The cone-like fruit is short-stalked, dark brown, and woody, and often remains on the tree during winter.

leaf to 10cm long

SMALL *flowers are borne in catkins; the males pendulous and yellow, females small, upright, and red.*

fruit to 1.5cm long

spreading habit

HEIGHT *10m.* **SPREAD** *10m.*
BARK *Dark grey and smooth.*
FLOWERING TIME *Early spring.*
OCCURRENCE *Cultivated and, in C. Europe, sometimes naturalized; native to Canada and N.E. USA.*
SIMILAR SPECIES *Grey Alder (above), which has more sharply toothed leaves, grey below.*

Yellow Birch

Betula alleghaniensis (Betulaceae)

A deciduous, broadly columnar to spreading tree, the Yellow Birch has hairy young shoots that smell of wintergreen when scratched. The alternate, oval, taper-pointed, finely toothed leaves are matt, dark green above, paler beneath, and turn yellow in autumn. Tiny flowers are borne in catkins: the males large, drooping, and yellow; the smaller females upright and reddish green. The small brown fruit in cylindrical, upright clusters, up to 3cm long, break up when mature.

YELLOW-BROWN in colour, the bark peels horizontally in thin, flaky strips.

columnar to spreading habit

toothed margin

leaf to 10cm long

male catkin to 10cm long

HEIGHT *20m.* **SPREAD** *15m.*
BARK *Yellow-brown, peels in horizontal strips.*
FLOWERING TIME *Early spring.*
OCCURRENCE *Cultivated; native to N.E. North America.*
SIMILAR SPECIES *Sweet Birch (Betula lenta), which has aromatic foliage, but the bark is dark red-brown and does not peel.*

Erman Birch

Betula ermanii (Betulaceae)

The young shoots of this deciduous, broadly conical tree are rough with small, glossy warts. Its alternate, oval, coarsely toothed leaves are taper-pointed, and glossy green above. The male catkins are drooping and yellow, the smaller females are upright and green. Small brown fruit clusters, up to 3cm long, break up when ripe.

conical habit

CREAMY white, with horizontal lenticels, the bark peels in papery strips.

toothed margin

leaf to 7.5cm long

fruiting catkin

male catkin to 10cm long

HEIGHT *25m.* **SPREAD** *15m.*
BARK *White with obvious, horizontal lenticels, peeling to reveal creamy to pink inner bark.*
FLOWERING TIME *Mid-spring.*
OCCURRENCE *Cultivated; native to N.E. Asia and Japan.*
SIMILAR SPECIES *Himalayan Birch (p.114), has sharper-toothed leaves and hairy shoots.*

River Birch

Betula nigra (Betulaceae)

This deciduous tree is conical when young, later becoming broadly columnar to spreading. Its blue-green leaves turn yellow in autumn, and taper to the base and the tip, giving them a diamond-shaped outline; they are deeply double-toothed above the middle. The female catkins are small, upright, and green, while the large male catkins are drooping and yellow. The small brown fruit are in cylindrical, upright clusters, up to 4cm long, and scatter on ripening.

PINK-GREY *bark peels in papery layers, and becomes dark brown and ridged on old trees.*

leaf to 10cm long

female catkin

male catkin to 7.5cm long

spreading habit

HEIGHT *15m.*
SPREAD *15m.*
BARK *Cream to pink-grey; brown with age.*
FLOWERING TIME *Mid-spring.*
OCCURRENCE *Cultivated; native to E. North America.*
SIMILAR SPECIES *None – this species has highly distinctive foliage and bark.*

Paper Birch

Betula papyrifera (Betulaceae)

Also known as Canoe Birch, this deciduous, fast-growing, conical tree has young shoots that are warty and often hairy. The matt, dark green, oval leaves are sharply toothed and taper to a point at the tip, turning yellow in autumn. The yellow male flowers are in drooping catkins; the green female flowers in upright to spreading catkins. Cylindrical, drooping clusters of brown fruit, up to 5cm long, break up as they ripen.

WHITE *with dark lenticels, the bark peels in horizontal strips, exposing a pinkish orange inner bark.*

leaf to 10cm long

conical habit

male catkin to 10cm long

HEIGHT *20m.* **SPREAD** *15m.*
BARK *White with horizontal lenticels.*
FLOWERING TIME *Mid-spring.*
OCCURRENCE *Cultivated; native to Canada and N. USA.*
SIMILAR SPECIES *Silver Birch (p.112), which has more sharply toothed leaves and white bark with dark cracks at the base.*

Silver Birch

Betula pendula (Betulaceae)

This large, deciduous tree has gracefully weeping branches. The young shoots are rough to the touch, with numerous small warts. Glossy and dark green, the leaves turn yellow in autumn. They are oval to triangular and edged with prominent double teeth. Tiny flowers are borne in catkins, the males yellow and drooping, and the green females upright, later drooping. The brown fruit clusters break up when ripe. Several selections are grown in gardens, such as 'Laciniata' with finely cut leaves and 'Tristis' with very pendulous shoots.

WHITE *bark of mature trees is prominently marked with dark scars, has deep cracks and knobbly bumps towards the base, and becomes black at the base on old trees.*

NOTE

The Silver Birch is the only birch species with a naturally pendulous habit compared to other Betula trees, giving it an easily recognizable form.

narrow, weeping habit

fruit cluster to 3cm long

leaf to 6cm long

female catkin

male catkin to 6cm long

HEIGHT *30m.* **SPREAD** *20m.*
BARK *White, often developing diamond-shaped, black markings at the base of mature trees.*
FLOWERING TIME *Mid-spring.*
OCCURRENCE *Woodlands, heaths, and mountains in Europe.*
SIMILAR SPECIES *Downy Birch (right), the other common birch of Europe, which has hairy shoots and leaves; the bark lacks the dark markings at the base of the trunk and remains white even on old trees.*

Grey Birch

Betula populifolia (Betulaceae)

A small, narrowly conical, deciduous tree, the Grey Birch has hairless, warty shoots. The oval, sharply toothed, glossy, dark green leaves are borne on slender stalks and end in long, tapered points. Tiny flowers are borne in catkins, the males drooping and yellow, the females smaller, upright, and green. The spreading, cylindrical clusters of small brown fruit, up to 3cm long, break up when mature.

WHITE *or grey-white bark has black marks and long lenticels; it darkens at the base with age, but does not peel.*

narrow, conical habit

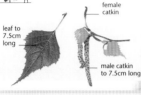

female catkin

leaf to 7.5cm long

male catkin to 7.5cm long

HEIGHT *10m.*
SPREAD *4m.*
BARK *White or grey-white, does not peel.*
FLOWERING TIME *Mid-spring.*
OCCURRENCE *Cultivated; native to E. North America.*
SIMILAR SPECIES *Silver Birch (left), is larger with black marks at the base on old trees.*

Downy Birch

Betula pubescens (Betulaceae)

Softly hairy young shoots and leaves give this conical, deciduous tree its name. Its broadly oval, dark green leaves, edged with single teeth, turn smooth and yellow in autumn. Tiny flowers are borne in catkins, the males drooping and yellow, the females smaller, upright, and green. The upright, cylindrical clusters of small brown fruit, up to 3cm long, break up when ripe.

conical habit

WHITE *bark may have grey or pinkish cracks at the base; it stays white at the base even on old trees.*

female catkin

fruiting catkin

male catkin to 10cm long

leaf to 6cm long

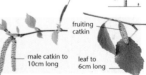

HEIGHT *20m.* **SPREAD** *12m.*
BARK *White, sometimes with grey or pinkish cracks at the base.*
FLOWERING TIME *Mid-spring.*
OCCURRENCE *Woodland, moors, and mountains in Europe.*
SIMILAR SPECIES *Silver Birch (left), has warty, hairless shoots and double-toothed leaves.*

Himalayan Birch

Betula utilis (Betulaceae)

This deciduous tree with a conical to columnar crown has silky, hairy young shoots. The often glossy, dark green, broadly oval, alternate leaves taper at the tip, are sharply toothed, and turn yellow in autumn. Tiny flowers are borne in catkins: the males yellow and drooping, the females smaller, green, and upright. The cylindrical clusters, to 3cm long, of small brown fruit, break up when mature.

PINKISH *white to coppery brown, the flaky bark makes this a popular ornamental tree.*

conical to columnar crown

fruiting catkin

leaf to 10cm long

male catkin to 12cm long

female catkin

HEIGHT *20m.* **SPREAD** *15m.*
BARK *Pinkish white to coppery brown.*
FLOWERING TIME *Mid-spring.*
OCCURRENCE *Cultivated; native to the Himalayas and W. China.*
SIMILAR SPECIES *Erman Birch (p.110), which has shoots that are hairless or nearly so, with many warts.*

Indian Bean Tree

Catalpa bignonioides (Bignoniaceae)

A deciduous, wide-spreading tree with stout shoots, the Indian Bean Tree has large, rather light green, broadly ovate, untoothed leaves, arranged in whorls of three on long stalks. The flowers at the ends of the shoots are followed by slender, hanging, bean-like pods, which ripen from green to brown and persist on the tree over winter. 'Aurea' is a selection with bright yellow young foliage.

CONICAL *clusters of bell-shaped white flowers have yellow and purple spots.*

spreading habit

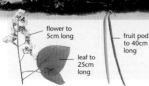
flower to 5cm long

fruit pod to 40cm long

leaf to 25cm long

HEIGHT *15m.*
SPREAD *20m.*
BARK *Grey and scaly.*
FLOWERING TIME *Midsummer.*
OCCURRENCE *Cultivated; native to S.E. USA.*
SIMILAR SPECIES *Empress Tree (p.205), which has opposite leaves densely covered in sticky hairs.*

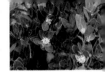

Balearic Box

Buxus balearica (Buxaceae)

Of conical to columnar habit, often low-growing and shrubby, particularly in very dry places, this evergreen tree has square young shoots. The opposite, leathery leaves are oval and dark green. The tiny green flowers are petal-less, males and females separate on the same plant. The male flowers have conspicuous yellow anthers. The small green fruit are about 8mm long and topped with three horns, which are nearly as long as the fruit.

WITH *their yellow anthers, the male flowers are showier than females.*

leaf to 4cm long

conical to columnar habit

HEIGHT *10m.*
SPREAD *5m or less.*
BARK *Pale grey-brown.*
FLOWERING TIME *Early spring.*
OCCURRENCE *Dry, rocky hillsides of S. Spain, Balearic Islands, and Sardinia.*
SIMILAR SPECIES *Common Box (below), has smaller leaves and a wider distribution.*

Common Box

Buxus sempervirens (Buxaceae)

This is evergreen plant is more often a shrub than a tree. Its opposite, dark green leaves are often blue-green when young. The flowers of both sexes are separate but in the same cluster, the males with conspicuous yellow anthers. The small green fruit are topped with three horns, which are much shorter than the fruit.

OFTEN *a shrub, particularly in exposed positions, but can become a tree in sheltered woodland.*

conical to columnar or spreading habit

leaf to 3cm long

male flowers

fruit to 8mm long

HEIGHT *6m.* SPREAD *5m.*
BARK *Grey and smooth, cracking into small squares on older trees.*
FLOWERING TIME *Early spring.*
OCCURRENCE *Scrub and woodland, usually on alkaline soils, throughout Europe.*
SIMILAR SPECIES *Balearic Box (above), which has larger leaves.*

Spindle Tree

Euonymus europaeus (Celastraceae)

FOUR-LOBED, *bright pink fruit, up to 1.2cm wide, open to reveal orange seeds.*

This often low-branching or shrubby, spreading, deciduous tree has green shoots ending in small leaf buds, to 5mm long. The dark green, opposite leaves are oval to lance-shaped and edged with fine teeth. They turn orange-red or purple in autumn. The tiny, greenish white flowers, each with four petals, open in small clusters, males and females separately, sometimes on different plants.

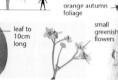

orange autumn foliage

leaf to 10cm long

small greenish flowers

HEIGHT *6m.* **SPREAD** *8m.*
BARK *Grey and smooth, fissured with age.*
FLOWERING TIME *Late spring to early summer.*
OCCURRENCE *Scrub, woodland, and hedgerows throughout Europe.*
SIMILAR SPECIES *Broad-leaved Spindle Tree (below), which has much larger buds.*

Broad-leaved Spindle Tree

Euonymus latifolius (Celastraceae)

NODDING *clusters of bright pink fruit split when ripe to reveal orange seeds.*

This deciduous, spreading tree is often shrubby and its shoots end in prominent, slender, and pointed buds, about 1cm long. The opposite, dark green leaves, up to 15cm long, are oval to oblong and edged with fine teeth. They turn reddish purple in autumn. The small pink flowers have five petals and are borne in clusters. The showy pink fruit have four narrow wings.

leaf to 15cm long

shrubby habit

fruit to 2cm wide

HEIGHT *6m.* **SPREAD** *8m.*
BARK *Grey and smooth.*
FLOWERING TIME *Late spring to early summer.*
OCCURRENCE *Woods and thickets of S. and S.E. Europe and Turkey.*
SIMILAR SPECIES *Spindle Tree (above), which has smaller buds.*

Katsura Tree

Cercidiphyllum japonicum (Cercidiphyllaceae)

This fast-growing, deciduous tree of conical to rounded habit, produces slender young shoots. The rounded, blue-green leaves are opposite or nearly so, edged with fine teeth, and heart-shaped at the base. Fallen leaves have a characteristic aroma of burnt sugar. The tiny petalless flowers emerge early in the year on bare shoots, males and females on separate plants. Male flowers have numerous red stamens. The female trees bear small, green, pod-like fruit clustered along the shoots.

ROUNDED, *blue-green leaves emerge early in the year, turning yellow to orange and purple in autumn.*

conical to rounded habit

yellow autumn foliage

NOTE

The name Cercidiphyllum refers to the resemblance of the leaves to those of the Judas Tree (p.147).

HEIGHT 20m.
SPREAD 20m.
BARK Pale grey-brown with shallow fissures, flaking on old trees.
FLOWERING TIME Early spring.
OCCURRENCE Cultivated; native to the Himalayas, China, and Japan.
SIMILAR SPECIES Judas Tree (p.147), which has alternate, rather than opposite, leaves that are not toothed.

leaf to 8cm wide

female flowers

Flowering Dogwood

Cornus florida (Cornaceae)

OPPOSITE, *oval leaves colour richly in autumn, from dark green above, greenish white and hairy beneath, to orange and red or purple.*

leaf to 10cm long

white bracts

The young shoots of this small, deciduous tree are covered with a blue-white bloom. Dense clusters of tiny greenish flowers open with the young leaves, each cluster surrounded by four conspicuous bracts, which are usually white but occasionally pink, and are notched at the tip. The egg-shaped, glossy red fruit, up to 1.5cm long, form in clusters, separating when ripe. Cultivated selections may have variegated foliage or pink to deep pink bracts.

spreading habit

HEIGHT *10m.* **SPREAD** *10m.*
BARK *Dark red-brown, cracking into small square plates on mature trees.*
FLOWERING TIME *Late spring.*
OCCURRENCE *Cultivated; native to E. North America.*
SIMILAR SPECIES *Japanese Strawberry Tree (below), Pacific Dogwood (right).*

Japanese Strawberry Tree

Cornus kousa (Cornaceae)

FLESHY *red fruit hang in clusters on long, slender stalks in autumn.*

The leaves of this deciduous, broadly conical to columnar tree are opposite, oval, dark green, and wavy-edged, the undersides with tufts of brown hairs in the axils of the veins. Tiny, long-stalked, greenish white flowers in dense clusters appear after the leaves emerge, each cluster surrounded by four conspicuous, creamy white or pink-tinged bracts. The red, strawberry-like fruit clusters are up to 2.5cm wide.

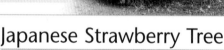

broadly columnar habit

clusters of flowers

4 taper-pointed bracts

leaf to 7.5cm long

HEIGHT *10m.* **SPREAD** *8m.*
BARK *Red-brown, flaking in patches.*
FLOWERING TIME *Early summer.*
OCCURRENCE *Cultivated; native to E. North America.*
SIMILAR SPECIES *Flowering Dogwood (above), whose fruit is not fleshy; C. kousa var. chinensis, which has larger leaves.*

Cornelian Cherry

Cornus mas (Cornaceae)

A deciduous, spreading tree or, more often, a shrub,
Cornelian Cherry has opposite, oval, dark green leaves.
Small flower buds are visible on the shoots during winter
and open in clusters before the leaves emerge. The edible,
fleshy, bright red fruit, up to 2cm long, each with a single
stone, are borne in clusters. Garden selections are
sometimes grown for their larger fruit or variegated foliage.

CLUSTERS *of
unpleasantly scented
tiny, four-petalled
yellow flowers open
before the leaves.*

shrubby
habit

leaf to
10cm
long

HEIGHT *10m.*
SPREAD *10m.*
BARK *Grey-brown and flaky.*
FLOWERING TIME *Late winter to
early spring.*
OCCURRENCE *Woodland edges and thickets
in C. and S.E. Europe.*
SIMILAR SPECIES *None.*

Pacific Dogwood

Cornus nuttallii (Cornaceae)

This deciduous, conical tree has opposite, oval, dark green
leaves, which turn yellow or red in autumn. The flowers
are borne in dense clusters as the leaves appear. They are
surrounded by six (sometimes four or eight) large, creamy
white or pinkish bracts. The flowerhead can grow up to
15cm wide. The egg-shaped red fruit, up to
1.5cm long, are borne in clusters,
which break up when ripe.

TINY, *greenish white
flower clusters are
surrounded by usually
six showy bracts.*

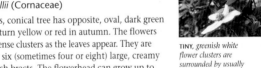

leaf to 15cm long

reddish
autumn
foliage

HEIGHT *15m.* **SPREAD** *10m.*
BARK *Grey and smooth.*
FLOWERING TIME *Late spring.*
OCCURRENCE *Cultivated; native to
W. North America.*
SIMILAR SPECIES *Flowering Dogwood (left),
which is smaller and has flowerheads with
only four bracts, notched at the tip.*

Dove Tree

Davidia involucrata (Cornaceae)

Showy white bracts around clusters of small flowers make this deciduous, broadly conical tree easily recognizable. Also known as the Ghost or Handkerchief Tree, large, bright red buds make this tree conspicuous in winter. Its stout shoots have heart-shaped leaves, dark green above and covered with white hair below. The round green fruit, 2.5cm wide, ripen to purple-brown.

ROUNDED *clusters of tiny flowers are surrounded by two showy white bracts.*

leaf to 15cm long

broadly conical habit

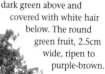

bract to 20cm long

HEIGHT *15m.*
SPREAD *10m.*
BARK *Orange-brown, peeling in small flakes on mature trees.*
FLOWERING TIME *Late spring.*
OCCURRENCE *Cultivated; native to China.*
SIMILAR SPECIES *None – no other tree shares similar features.*

Tupelo

Nyssa sylvatica (Cornaceae)

Variously known as Black Gum, Sour Gum, or Tupelo, this deciduous tree has a broadly conical to columnar crown and slender, spreading branches. Variable in shape, the smooth, untoothed, dark green and often glossy leaves are clustered on shoots. The flowers open in small, rounded clusters on slender stalks. Bunches of berry-like, egg-shaped, blue-black fruit, up to 1cm long, ripen in autumn.

BRIGHT *red or yellow leaves in autumn makes this one of the finest trees for rich seasonal colour.*

ovate to elliptic leaves

tiny green flowers

broadly conical to columnar habit

HEIGHT *20m.*
SPREAD *15m.*
BARK *Dark grey-brown, deeply ridged and furrowed on older trees.*
FLOWERING TIME *Spring.*
OCCURRENCE *Cultivated; native to E. North America.*
SIMILAR SPECIES *None.*

Hornbeam

Carpinus betulus (Betulaceae)

Conical when young, the deciduous Hornbeam develops a more rounded outline, the slender shoots often drooping at the tips. The oval to oblong leaves have prominent veins and are sharply double-toothed at the margins. They are dark green above, paler beneath, and turn yellow in autumn. The tiny flowers are borne in pendulous catkins as the young leaves emerge; males are yellow-brown, females are green and shorter. Small fruit, in hanging clusters, ripen from green to yellow-brown, each hidden at the base of a conspicuous bract with three untoothed lobes.

PENDULOUS *fruiting clusters, which are made conspicuous by their three-lobed green bracts, are borne in summer.*

broadly spreading habit

leaf to 10cm long

male catkin to 5cm long

female catkin

fruit cluster to 7.5cm long

HEIGHT *30m.* **SPREAD** *25m.*
BARK *Pale grey and smooth, fluted on old trees.*
FLOWERING TIME *Early spring.*
OCCURRENCE *Deciduous woodlands and commonly in hedgerows, all over Europe.*
SIMILAR SPECIES *Oriental Hornbeam (p.122), the only other* Carpinus *species native to Europe, which is a much smaller tree or shrub;* *Hop Hornbeam (p.124), which has rough bark and hop-like fruit.*

NOTE

A Hornbeam without fruit can be identified by its fluted trunk. When used in hedges, this species can be recognized by its sharply double-toothed leaves which are folded along the veins.

Oriental Hornbeam

Carpinus orientalis (Betulaceae)

SMOOTH *purple-grey bark, gradually becomes fluted on older trees.*

Often shrubby and forming thickets, this deciduous tree has alternate, sharply-toothed leaves that turn yellow in autumn. Tiny flowers are borne in pendulous catkins as the young leaves emerge; the males are yellow-brown, to 5cm long, females shorter and green. The fruit is a small nut, about 4mm long, hidden at the base of leaf-like, sharply toothed bracts, in pendulous clusters, ripening to yellow-brown.

spreading habit

dark green leaves

leaf to 5cm long

HEIGHT *20m.* SPREAD *15m.*
BARK *Purplish grey, smooth.*
FLOWERING TIME *Early spring.*
OCCURRENCE *Deciduous woodland and thickets from S.E. Europe to the Caucasus.*
SIMILAR SPECIES *Hornbeam (p.121), which is a larger tree with larger leaves and 3-lobed bracts.*

Common Hazel

Corylus avellana (Betulaceae)

PALE *yellow pendulous catkins hang from bare shoots, and contain the male flowers.*

Frequently shrubby and forming thickets, this spreading tree has several stems from the base and is often coppiced for its shoots. The alternate, heart-shaped, hairy, dark green leaves turn yellow in autumn. Male flowers appear before the leaves open and female flowers are tiny, with only the red stigmas showing. Partially enclosed in a deeply lobed pale green husk, the edible nuts (cobnuts) are carried in clusters of up to four.

multiple stems

leaf to 10cm long

edible nuts

HEIGHT *10m.* SPREAD *10m.*
BARK *Grey-brown, glossy, peeling in strips.*
FLOWERING TIME *Late winter to early spring.*
OCCURRENCE *Woodlands and their margins, and thickets; throughout Europe.*
SIMILAR SPECIES *Filbert (right), has fruit in a tubular husk; Turkish Hazel (right), has a slender-pointed, toothed, lobed husk.*

Turkish Hazel

Corylus colurna (Betulaceae)

This deciduous tree with a compact, conical head has young shoots covered in sticky hairs. Before the alternate, broadly oval, dark green leaves open, the male flowers hang in pendulous, pale yellow catkins from the bare shoots. Female flowers are tiny, with only the red stigmas showing. The edible nuts are in clusters, each enclosed in pale green husk with long, tapered lobes.

COARSELY *double-toothed leaves are heart-shaped at the base; fruit are in deeply-lobed bracts.*

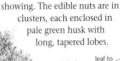

conical head

leaf to 15cm long

male catkin to 10cm long

HEIGHT *25m.* **SPREAD** *15m.*
BARK *Grey-brown, flaking in small plates.*
FLOWERING TIME *Late winter to early spring.*
OCCURRENCE *Deciduous woodlands of S.E. Europe; frequently planted in parks and streets.*
SIMILAR SPECIES *Common Hazel (left) and Filbert (below), which are generally smaller.*

Filbert

Corylus maxima (Betulaceae)

Usually with several main stems and more often a shrub, this spreading, deciduous tree has alternate, dark green leaves that turn yellow in autumn. Male flowers open in pale yellow, pendulous catkins before the leaves; females are tiny, with only the red stigmas showing. The edible fruit are in clusters, each enclosed in a tubular pale green husk. 'Purpurea', with purple foliage, is sometimes seen in gardens.

HEART-*shaped, dark green leaves have a double-toothed margin and are carried on hairy stalks.*

leaf to 12cm long

fruit in tubular husk

male catkin to 8cm long

HEIGHT *10m.*
SPREAD *10m.*
BARK *Grey-brown.*
FLOWERING TIME *Late winter to early spring.*
OCCURRENCE *Woodlands and thickets of S.E. Europe; cultivated for its edible nuts.*
SIMILAR SPECIES *Common Hazel (left), has a shorter husk which does not hide the nut.*

Hop Hornbeam

Ostrya carpinifolia (Corylaceae)

A distinguishing feature of this deciduous tree is its hop-like fruit clusters. These have creamy white husks that completely enclose the small nuts. The alternate, oval leaves, which are finely toothed at the margin, end in a short, tapered point. They are matt, dark green above, paler beneath, and turn yellow in autumn. Tiny male and female flowers are borne in separate catkins; male catkins are pendulous and yellow, while the females are shorter and green.

DISTINCTIVE, *hop-like fruit clusters composed of inflated, creamy white husks make an attractive feature as they ripen during summer.*

broadly conical to spreading habit

matt, dark green foliage

leaf to 10cm long

fruit to 5cm long

male catkin to 8cm long

NOTE

This tree derives its common name from its hop-like fruit clusters and from its resemblance to the Hornbeam (p.121), which has similar leaves and wood.

HEIGHT *20m.*
SPREAD *15m.*
BARK *Grey-brown and smooth when young; flaking on older trees.*
FLOWERING TIME *Spring.*
OCCURRENCE *Deciduous woodland of S. Europe.*
SIMILAR SPECIES *Hornbeam (p.121), which has smooth bark, and produces nuts surrounded by three-lobed bracts.*

Kaki

Diospyros kaki (Ebenaceae)

This is a deciduous tree with a spreading to columnar head. The alternate, glossy, dark green leaves are oval with a pointed tip and untoothed margin and turn red or orange in autumn. The bell-shaped yellow flowers, about 1.5cm long, have four sepal lobes, which persist on the fruit. Male and female flowers are borne on separate trees, the males in small clusters, the females singly.

JUICY, *tomato-like, edible fruit are yellow to orange or red, and have pointed tips.*

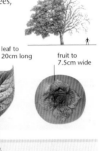

orange-red autumn foliage

leaf to 20cm long

fruit to 7.5cm wide

HEIGHT *14m.*
SPREAD *12m.*
BARK *Grey and scaly; fissured with age.*
FLOWERING TIME *Summer.*
OCCURRENCE *Cultivated for its edible fruit, especially in warm areas; native to China.*
SIMILAR SPECIES *Date Plum (below), which has much smaller fruit and is a larger tree.*

Date Plum

Diospyros lotus (Ebenaceae)

Deciduous, with a spreading to columnar head, the Date Plum has alternate, untoothed, glossy, dark green leaves that are lance-shaped, elliptical, or oval, and end in a tapered point. The bell-shaped, pink to orange-yellow flowers are four-lobed. Male and female flowers are borne on separate trees, the males in small clusters, the females singly. The rounded, edible fruit end in a point and ripen from green to orange-yellow or blue-black.

SMOOTH *and grey when young, the bark turns dark with age, fissuring into square plates.*

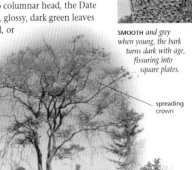

spreading crown

HEIGHT *20m.* **SPREAD** *15m.*
BARK *Grey and smooth; becomes dark and cracks into square plates with age.*
FLOWERING TIME *Summer.*
OCCURRENCE *Cultivated and sometimes naturalized in S. Europe; native to Turkey, S.W. Asia, and N. Iran.*
SIMILAR SPECIES *Kaki (above) has larger fruit.*

female flower about 5mm long

leaf to 15cm long

fruit 2cm wide

Oleaster

Elaeagnus angustifolia (Elaeagnaceae)

ROUGH, *red-brown bark becomes fissured and scaly, shredding with age.*

• Also known as Russian Olive, this broadly conical to spreading, deciduous tree has spiny shoots covered in silver scales. The alternate, willow-like leaves are narrowly oblong to lance-shaped and are dark green above and silvery with scales beneath. Clusters of small, fragrant, bell-shaped yellow flowers open in the axils of the young leaves. The egg-shaped yellow to reddish fruit, up to 2cm long, are edible.

fragrant yellow flowers

silvery green foliage

leaf to 8cm long

HEIGHT *12m.* **SPREAD** *10m.*
BARK *Red-brown, fissured, and scaly.*
FLOWERING TIME *Late spring to early summer.*
OCCURRENCE *Cultivated; often naturalized in S. and C. Europe; native to W. and C. Asia.*
SIMILAR SPECIES *Sea Buckthorn (below), has smaller leaves and rounded orange fruit.*

Sea Buckthorn

Hippophae rhamnoides (Elaeagnaceae)

ROUNDED, *fleshy, bright orange fruit are densely clustered along the shoots.*

This deciduous, thicket-forming shrub or small tree, with spiny shoots, spreads by suckers from the base. Its alternate, slender, linear, untoothed leaves are covered in silver scales on both sides. Tiny yellowish flowers open in small clusters before or as the leaves emerge, with males and females on separate plants. It is frequently planted as an ornamental tree and to stabilize sand dunes.

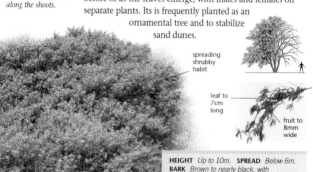

spreading shrubby habit

leaf to 7cm long

fruit to 8mm wide

HEIGHT *Up to 10m.* **SPREAD** *Below 6m.*
BARK *Brown to nearly black, with vertical fissures.*
FLOWERING TIME *Spring.*
OCCURRENCE *Coastal regions, sandy soils, and riverbanks of N. and C. Europe.*
SIMILAR SPECIES *Oleaster (above), which has larger leaves and fruit.*

Grecian Strawberry Tree

Arbutus andrachne (Ericaceae)

This sometimes shrubby, evergreen, spreading tree has smooth red young shoots. The alternate, oval to oblong, leathery, dark green leaves are untoothed, or sometimes have occasional teeth on vigorous shoots. Small, urn-shaped white flowers, about 6mm long, are carried in upright clusters. The small, rounded, orange-red fruit are about 1cm wide and nearly smooth.

RED-BROWN *bark peels in thin strips to reveal a bright orange-brown layer beneath.*

broadly spreading habit

leaf to 10cm long

flower cluster to 10cm long

HEIGHT *10m.* **SPREAD** *10m.*
BARK *Red-brown, peeling in thin strips.*
FLOWERING TIME *Early spring.*
OCCURRENCE *Woods, thickets, and rocky slopes of S.E. Europe.*
SIMILAR SPECIES *Hybrid Strawberry Tree (below), has toothed leaves; Strawberry Tree (p.128), has bark that does not peel.*

Hybrid Strawberry Tree

Arbutus x andrachnoides (Ericaceae)

A naturally occurring hybrid between the Strawberry Tree (p.128) and the Grecian Strawberry Tree (above), this evergreen, spreading tree has red young shoots with some sticky hairs. The alternate, oval, glossy, dark green leaves are finely toothed. Small, urn-shaped white flowers, about 6mm long, are carried in nodding clusters. The orange-red, rounded fruit are about 1.5cm wide and rough with warts.

RED-BROWN, *the bark peels in long, thin, vertical strips with age*

open, spreading crown

leaf to 10cm long

flower cluster to 10cm long

HEIGHT *10m.* **SPREAD** *10m.*
BARK *Red-brown, peeling in thin strips.*
FLOWERING TIME *Spring or autumn.*
OCCURRENCE *Woods, thickets, and rocky slopes where the parents grow together; native to S.E. Europe.*
SIMILAR SPECIES *Strawberry Tree (p.128), Grecian Strawberry Tree (above).*

Strawberry Tree

Arbutus unedo (Ericaceae)

PENDULOUS and roughly warty on the surface, the fruit resemble small strawberries.

A spreading, evergreen tree, the Strawberry tree has sticky hairs on the young shoots. The alternate, oval leaves are glossy, dark green, with toothed margins. Small, urn-shaped white or, more rarely, pink flowers are borne in drooping clusters at the ends of the shoots as the fruit from the previous year's flowers are ripening. The very characteristic, strawberry-like fruit, which give the tree its name, ripen from green through yellow to red. Unlike many members of its family, this tree can often be found growing on alkaline soil. Some forms have untoothed leaves. There are famous stands of this tree in W. Ireland (Cork, Killarney, and Sligo).

broadly spreading habit

glossy green foliage

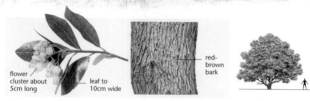

flower cluster about 5cm long

leaf to 10cm wide

red-brown bark

HEIGHT *10m.* **SPREAD** *10m.*
BARK *Red-brown, rough, and flaking but not peeling.*
FLOWERING TIME *Autumn.*
OCCURRENCE *Thickets and woodland in rocky places in the Mediterranean region and S.W. Ireland; a popular ornamental tree in gardens.*
SIMILAR SPECIES *Grecian Strawberry Tree (p.127), which has untoothed leaves; Hybrid Strawberry Tree (p.127), which has toothed leaves.*

NOTE

"Unedo" means literally "I eat one", referring to the fact that the fruit is edible, although it is not exactly delicious.

Tree Heath

Erica arborea (Ericaceae)

This evergreen tree, with an upright to spreading head, usually has several main stems and is often shrubby. The slender, needle-like, bright green leaves, to 5mm long, are densely arranged in whorls of three or four on the upright, hairy shoots. Carried on the short side shoots, the small, short-stalked, honey-scented flowers are white, fading to brown. The fruit are small, brown, and dry, containing many tiny seeds. Several forms are cultivated in gardens; a shrubby form, *E. arborea* var. *alpina,* is grown in gardens for its ability to withstand hard frost.

SMALL, *fragrant, bell-shaped white flowers, about 3mm long, are densely arranged on numerous short side shoots, forming long, slender spikes.*

pyramidal spikes

flower to 3mm long

shrubby, spreading habit

NOTE

Traditionally, wood from the roots of this tree was used to make briar pipes in S. Europe; briar comes from bruyère, French for plants.

HEIGHT *6m or more.*
SPREAD *4m.*
BARK *Grey-brown, flaking in thin vertical strips.*
FLOWERING TIME *Early to mid-spring.*
OCCURRENCE *Thickets and mountain slopes of S. Europe.*
SIMILAR SPECIES *The shrubby E. lusitanica is similar but the flowers have a red stigma; Spanish Heath (E. australis), which has purple flowers.*

Spanish Chestnut

Castanea sativa (Fagaceae)

SLENDER, *creamy white flower spikes cover the tree in summer, making for a spectacular sight in parks and gardens.*

Also known as the Sweet Chestnut, this deciduous tree was widely introduced outside its native region of southern Europe by the Romans. Large and vigorous, it has stout shoots and a broadly columnar head. Its alternate, oblong leaves taper to a point and are edged with numerous slender-pointed teeth. They are glossy, dark green and turn yellow-brown in autumn. The flowers are borne in long, slender, upright to spreading catkins. The pale green fruit husk, densely covered with slender, sharp spines, encloses up to three glossy brown, edible nuts.

catkin to 25cm long

leaf to 20cm long

nuts in spiny husk

broadly columnar habit

HEIGHT *30m.* **SPREAD** *20m.*
BARK *Grey and smooth; brown with spiralling ridges on older specimens.*
FLOWERING TIME *Midsummer.*
OCCURRENCE *Woodland with acid soil in S. Europe; frequently planted and often naturalized.*
SIMILAR SPECIES *Horse Chestnut (p.65), which has superficially similar fruit, but larger flower clusters and opposite leaves.*

Oriental Beech

Fagus orientalis (Fagaceae)

A deciduous tree, the Oriental Beech is conical when young, later becoming broadly columnar to spreading. Its alternate, dark green leaves are widest above the middle and have up to 12 pairs of veins. Tiny flowers open in clusters, males and females separate; the males are more conspicuous, in rounded, pale yellow heads. The fruit is a woody husk with one or two edible nuts.

leaf to 12cm long

fruit 2.5cm long

4-lobed husk

broad habit

WAVY-EDGED and dark green, the leaves are silky when young, turning yellow-brown in autumn.

HEIGHT *30m.*
SPREAD *20m.*
BARK *Pale grey and smooth, sometimes furrowed.*
FLOWERING TIME *Mid-spring.*
OCCURRENCE *Woodlands of S.E. Europe.*
SIMILAR SPECIES *Common Beech (below), which has smaller leaves.*

Common Beech

Fagus sylvatica (Fagaceae)

Zig-zag shoots ending in long, slender-pointed buds characterize this spreading, deciduous tree. It has alternate, dark green, wavy-edged leaves, widest above the middle, with up to ten pairs of veins. Its tiny flowers open with the young leaves, males and females in separate clusters. The more conspicuous males are borne in drooping, rounded, pale yellow heads. The fruit is a woody husk, up to 2.5cm long, and contains one or two edible nuts.

SILKY and hairy when young, the dark green leaves turn bright yellow in autumn.

spreading habit

leaf to 10cm long

yellow autumn foliage

HEIGHT *30m.*
SPREAD *20m.*
BARK *Pale grey and smooth.*
FLOWERING TIME *Mid-spring.*
OCCURRENCE *Woodland, on alkaline and well-drained soils, throughout Europe.*
SIMILAR SPECIES *Oriental Beech (above), which has larger leaves.*

Rauli

Nothofagus alpina (Fagaceae)

OBLONG, *finely toothed leaves are made distinctive by the numerous parallel veins.*

This deciduous tree has a broadly columnar head and slender shoots, which are hairy when young. The matt, dark green leaves, paler beneath, are bronze when young; each has up to 18 pairs of parallel veins and hairy on both sides. Flowers are tiny and greenish, male and female borne in separate clusters. The fruit has a green husk up to 1cm long, which is brown when ripe, covered with sticky bristles, and contains three small nuts.

broadly columnar habit

leaf to 10cm long

HEIGHT *25m.* **SPREAD** *15m.*
BARK *Grey-green and dark grey; fissured on old trees.*
FLOWERING TIME *Late spring.*
OCCURRENCE *Cultivated; native to Chile and Argentina.*
SIMILAR SPECIES *Roble (below), which has fewer veins on its leaves.*

Roble

Nothofagus obliqua (Fagaceae)

SMOOTH *and grey when young, the bark begins to crack and flake with age.*

A deciduous tree with slender shoots, the Roble is conical when young, later becoming broadly columnar. Dark green and oval, the toothed leaves are blue-green beneath and turn yellow in autumn. They have up to ten pairs of veins. The tiny greenish flowers are insignificant, the males and females in separate clusters. The fruit has a scaly green husk, turns brown when ripe, and contains three small nuts.

leaf to 8cm long

conical to columnar habit

fruit to 1cm long

HEIGHT *30m.* **SPREAD** *20m.*
BARK *Grey and smooth when young; cracking into plates with age.*
FLOWERING TIME *Mid-spring.*
OCCURRENCE *Cultivated; native to Chile and Argentina.*
SIMILAR SPECIES *Rauli (above), which has larger leaves with more veins.*

Algerian Oak

Quercus canariensis (Fagaceae)

A semi-evergreen tree with a broadly columnar crown, this species retains at least some of its leaves until spring. The large leaves, widest above the middle, are on stalks up to 2.5cm long, and have untoothed lobes that decrease in size towards the leaf tip. They are dark green above and blue-green beneath with loose white hairs, which rub off easily. Only some leaves turn yellow or yellow-brown in autumn. The flowers are in catkins, with the males being yellow-green, pendulous, and 4cm long, while the females are inconspicuous. Short-stalked acorns, 2.5cm long, are held in a hairy cup and ripen in the first year.

CONICAL *buds, the scales edged with white hairs, tip the stout shoots.*

broadly columnar crown

leaf to 15cm long

dark green foliage

NOTE

In spite of its Latin name, which suggests this species might be associated with the Canary Islands, it is not native to these islands but to North Africa.

HEIGHT *25m.* **SPREAD** *15m.*
BARK *Dark grey and thick and with deep fissures.*
FLOWERING TIME *Late spring.*
OCCURRENCE *Woodlands, mainly on hills and mountains, in S. Spain and Portugal.*
SIMILAR SPECIES *Normally very distinct, but can be confused in gardens with its hybrids with English Oak (page 141) and Sessile Oak (p.139).*

Turkey Oak

Quercus cerris (Fagaceae)

DENSELY *covered in narrow, bristle-like scales, the acorn cup encloses half the acorn, which ripens in the second year.*

The hairy shoots of this large, vigorous, deciduous tree are tipped with leaf buds surrounded by characteristic long whisker-like stipules. Its alternate leaves are variable in shape, toothed, and deeply lobed, on stalks to 2cm long. They are dark green above, slightly rough, blue-green beneath, and hairy, at least when young. The flowers are borne in catkins, the males yellow-green and drooping, to 6cm long, the females inconspicuous and borne separately.

spreading habit

leaf to 12cm long

acorn to 2.5cm long

HEIGHT *35m.*
SPREAD *25m.*
BARK *Grey brown and deeply ridged.*
FLOWERING TIME *Early summer.*
OCCURRENCE *Woodland in S. and C. Europe; also widely planted and naturalized.*
SIMILAR SPECIES *Lucombe Oak (p.136), which is semi-evergreen.*

Kermes Oak

Quercus coccifera (Fagaceae)

RIGID, *spiky scales densely cover the cup carrying the 2.5cm-long acorn.*

An evergreen, bushy shrub, but sometimes a broadly columnar tree, Kermes Oak has alternate, rigid, holly-like leaves edged with sharp spines. It is very distinctive among oaks and often confused with holly. Bronze when young, the leaves mature to dark green and are glossy on both sides. The flowers are in catkins, the males yellow-brown and drooping, to 5cm long, the females inconspicuous. The acorns ripen in the second year.

shrubby or columnar habit

leaf to 4cm long

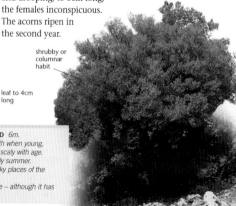

HEIGHT *10m.* **SPREAD** *6m.*
BARK *Dark grey, smooth when young, becoming cracked and scaly with age.*
FLOWERING TIME *Early summer.*
OCCURRENCE *Dry, rocky places of the Mediterranean region.*
SIMILAR SPECIES *None – although it has holly-like leaves.*

Scarlet Oak

Quercus coccinea (Fagaceae)

This deciduous, spreading tree has smooth shoots. The alternate leaves are toothed and deeply lobed, each lobe ending in slender, bristle-like tips, with small tufts of hair in the vein axils beneath. The flowers are in catkins: the males yellow-green and drooping, to 8cm long, the females inconspicuous, borne separately. The acorns are up to 2.5cm long, half enclosed in a glossy cup, and ripen the second year.

BRIGHT *red in autumn, the leaves are otherwise glossy dark green above, paler beneath.*

leaf to 15cm long

broadly spreading habit

HEIGHT *25m.* **SPREAD** *25m.*
BARK *Dark grey and smooth, later ridged.*
FLOWERING TIME *Late spring.*
OCCURRENCE *Cultivated; native to E. North America.*
SIMILAR SPECIES *Pin Oak (p.138), which has more conspicuous hair tufts under the leaf; Red Oak (p.142), which has dull leaves.*

Portuguese Oak

Quercus faginea (Fagaceae)

Semi-evergreen and spreading, this tree is sometimes low and shrubby. Its alternate leaves are glossy, dark green above, hairy beneath at first becoming smooth and blue-green. Flowers are borne in catkins, the males yellow-green and drooping, to 4cm long, the females inconspicuous. Acorns to 3.5cm long ripen in the first year. This variable species has several forms: subsp. *broteroi* has larger leaves which remain densely hairy beneath.

OVAL, *leathery, glossy dark green leaves are edged with rounded or slightly pointed teeth.*

spreading habit

leaf to 10cm long

blue-green underside

HEIGHT *20m.* **SPREAD** *15m.*
BARK *Dark grey; becoming scaly with age.*
FLOWERING TIME *Late spring.*
OCCURRENCE *Woodlands, hills, and river valleys of S.W. Spain and S. Portugal.*
SIMILAR SPECIES *Algerian Oak, (p.133) which has hairs on the undersides of young leaves that are easily rubbed off.*

Hungarian Oak

Quercus frainetto (Fagaceae)

DEEPLY *lobed leaves are clustered towards the end of the shoots, and turn yellow-brown in autumn.*

This large, deciduous tree has stout, slightly hairy shoots. Its oblong leaves have numerous blunt-tipped lobes, the larger ones sometimes notched, and are dark green above and grey-green beneath. The flowers are borne in catkins: the males yellow-green and pendulous, the females inconspicuous. The short-stalked acorns, up to 2cm long, ripen in the first year.

notched, larger lobe

leaf to 20cm long

broadly spreading habit

male catkin

HEIGHT *30m.*
SPREAD *25m.*
BARK *Dark grey, rugged, and deeply fissured.*
FLOWERING TIME *Late spring.*
OCCURRENCE *Woodland in S.E. Europe.*
SIMILAR SPECIES *None – its large, deeply lobed leaves make it highly distinctive.*

Lucombe Oak

Quercus x hispanica (Fagaceae)

GREY-BROWN *in colour, the bark can be corky in some forms, a feature inherited from the Cork Oak.*

A hybrid between Turkey Oak (p.134) and Cork Oak (p.143), this is a semi-evergreen tree. Its leaves are very variable in shape and size, and are edged with pointed teeth. They are glossy, dark green above and grey-white with hairs beneath. The flowers are borne in catkins, the males yellow-green and pendulous, the females inconspicuous. Acorns, up to 2cm long, in cups covered by bristly scales, ripen in the second year.

rounded top

leaf to 12cm long

HEIGHT *30m.* **SPREAD** *30m.*
BARK *Grey-brown, fissured, sometimes corky.*
FLOWERING TIME *Late spring.*
OCCURRENCE *Woodland, usually with the parent species; commonly cultivated; native to S. Europe.*
SIMILAR SPECIES *Turkey Oak (p.134), Cork Oak (p.143).*

Holm Oak

Quercus ilex (Fagaceae)

The young shoots of this large, evergreen tree are densely covered with grey-white hairs. The elliptic to narrowly ovate, leathery and rigid leaves are glossy, dark green above, closely covered with grey hairs beneath, and may be toothed or untoothed. They are very variable in shape on young plants, with a spiny margin. Young trees and shoots from the base of old trees often have sharply toothed leaves, like those of holly (*Ilex*), which are green beneath. The flowers are borne in catkins: the males, blooming on young shoots, are drooping, yellow-green and pendulous; the females, borne separately on the same plant, are small and inconspicuous. The acorns are held in cups up to one-third their length and they ripen in the first year.

PENDULOUS *catkins appear along with the grey young leaves, making this tree a showy sight in early summer.*

leaf to 10cm long

pointed acorn

acorn to 2cm long

dense, rounded head

spreading habit

HEIGHT *30m.* **SPREAD** *30m.*
BARK *Nearly black, cracking into small, scaly squares with age.*
FLOWERING TIME *Early summer.*
OCCURRENCE *Woods in hills and along coastal cliffs in the Mediterranean region; commonly planted and sometimes naturalized.*
SIMILAR SPECIES *Quercus rotundifolia (p.142), which has more rounded, blue-green leaves and larger, edible acorns; Cork Oak (p.143), which has corky bark.*

NOTE

In most regions, this is the most commonly cultivated evergreen oak tree. Often seen in coastal areas in its native regions, the Holm Oak has become widely naturalized in similar situations in southern England.

Valonia Oak

Quercus macrolepis (Fagaceae)

The young shoots of this deciduous or semi-evergreen tree are densely covered with white hairs. Edged with large teeth that end in bristle-like points, the alternate leaves are hairy on both sides when young, but only on the underside of mature dark green leaves. The flowers are borne in catkins; the males yellow-green and drooping, the females inconspicuous. Acorns ripen in the second year.

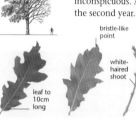

DENSE *scales cover the acorn cup containing the ripe 4cm-long fruit.*

bristle-like point

spreading head

white-haired shoot

leaf to 10cm long

HEIGHT *15m.*
SPREAD *12m.*
BARK *Dark grey; deeply fissured and cracked with age.*
FLOWERING TIME *Late spring.*
OCCURRENCE *Woodlands of S.E. Europe.*
SIMILAR SPECIES *Turkey Oak (p.134), which lacks the long bristle tips on the leaves.*

Pin Oak

Quercus palustris (Fagaceae)

DEEPLY *lobed red autumn leaves are glossy on both sides with conspicuous tufts of hair below.*

A deciduous tree with a broadly conical to spreading head, the lower branches of the Pin Oak droop distinctly. The alternate, glossy green leaves end in bristle-tipped teeth and have tufts of hair in the vein axils on their undersides. The flowers are borne in catkins; the males yellow-green and drooping, the females inconspicuous. The acorns ripen in the second year.

broadly conical habit

leaf to 15cm long

acorn about 1.5cm long

HEIGHT *30m.* **SPREAD** *25m.*
BARK *Grey and smooth.*
FLOWERING TIME *Late spring.*
OCCURRENCE *Cultivated; native to E. North America.*
SIMILAR SPECIES *Scarlet Oak (p.135), lacks the conspicuous hair tufts; Red Oak (p.142), has dull green leaves, blue-green beneath.*

Sessile Oak

Quercus petraea (Fagaceae)

This is a large, deciduous tree with a spreading head and smooth young shoots. The alternate leaves are borne on stalks to 1cm or more long and are edged with rounded, untoothed lobes. Dark, slightly glossy green above, they have a thin layer of hairs beneath. Male and female flowers are borne separately in catkins: the males yellow-green and drooping, to 8cm long; the females inconspicuous. Unstalked or very short-stalked, about one-third of the acorn is enclosed in a cup.

A variable and widely distributed species, the Sessile Oak has many garden selections varying in leaf shape.

PROMINENT *and deep vertical ridges develop on the grey bark of mature trees.*

broadly spreading habit

leaf to 12cm long

acorn to 3cm long

NOTE

Where this species grows alongside Common Oak (p.141), it hybridizes to form Q. x rosacea, with intermediate characters.

HEIGHT *40m.*
SPREAD *25m.*
BARK *Grey; vertically ridged in mature trees.*
FLOWERING TIME *Late spring.*
OCCURRENCE *Woodlands throughout Europe.*
SIMILAR SPECIES *English Oak (p.141), which has leaves with very short stalks but long-stalked acorns. Other deciduous European oaks tend to have hairy shoots and often much hairier leaves.*

Downy Oak

Quercus pubescens (Fagaceae)

SOFT *hairs cover the young shoots and grey-green leaves; the leaves become almost smooth as they mature.*

A variable and widely distributed, deciduous tree, this oak has a spreading head and hairy young shoots. The alternate leaves have up to eight rounded to pointed lobes on each side, and are softly hairy above and below when young. The flowers are borne in catkins: the males drooping and yellow-green, the females inconspicuous. Short-stalked acorns, to 4cm long, ripen in the first year.

leaf to 10cm long

dark grey-green mature leaves

spreading habit

HEIGHT *20m.* SPREAD *15m.*
BARK *Dark grey, deeply ridged, and cracked.*
FLOWERING TIME *Late spring.*
OCCURRENCE *Dry, sunny hillsides of S. and C. Europe.*
SIMILAR SPECIES *Sessile Oak (p.139), which has smooth shoots; Pyrenean Oak (below), which has leaves that are smooth above.*

Pyrenean Oak

Quercus pyrenaica (Fagaceae)

SHORT-STALKED *acorns, to 4cm long, with densely scaled caps ripen in the first year.*

This deciduous tree has a broadly columnar head and softly hairy shoots. Deeply cut into up to eight lobes on each side, the alternate leaves, widest above the middle, emerge late, becoming glossy dark green, and covered with white hairs beneath. The flowers are borne in catkins: the males yellow-green and the females inconspicuous.

spreading habit

leaf to 15cm long

drooping catkins

HEIGHT *20m.*
SPREAD *15m.*
BARK *Grey and cracked.*
FLOWERING TIME *Early summer.*
OCCURRENCE *Woods in the mountains of S.W. Europe.*
SIMILAR SPECIES *Downy Oak (above), which has less deeply lobed leaves.*

English Oak

Quercus robur (Fagaceae)

This oak is a deciduous, spreading tree with smooth shoots. The alternate, smooth, widest above the middle, very short-stalked leaves have 5–7 lobes on each side, and are dark green above and blue-green beneath. Where the base of the leaf meets the stalk, the blade is turned slightly upwards. Flowers are borne in catkins: the males yellow-green and drooping, the females inconspicuous. Several selections are grown in gardens such as 'Fastigiata' (Cypress Oak), which is narrowly columnar with upright branches, and 'Pendula', which has weeping branches.

LONG-STALKED *acorns are enclosed in a scaly cup. Initially green, they turn brown and may develop dark stripes; they ripen in the first year.*

rounded head

spreading habit

yellow-green male flowers

leaf up to 12cm long

acorn to 4cm long

HEIGHT *35m.*
SPREAD *30m.*
BARK *Grey with vertical fissures.*
FLOWERING TIME *Late spring.*
OCCURRENCE *Woods throughout Europe; especially common in W. Europe and throughout Britain.*
SIMILAR SPECIES *Sessile Oak (p.139), which has long-stalked leaves and unstalked acorns.*

NOTE

This is the commonest oak across much of Europe, but is found less often in the south. It can be up to 1,000 years old. The wood is used for wine casks.

Quercus rotundifolia

Quercus rotundifolia (Fagaceae)

An evergreen, spreading tree, *Q. rotundifolia* is closely related to Holm Oak (p.137). The alternate, leathery, and rounded leaves are spine-toothed on young plants but become oval and spineless as the tree matures. Male flowers are borne in drooping, yellow-green catkins; the females are inconspicuous. The large acorns, up to 4cm long, are sweet and edible, ripening the first year. Pigs fed on these acorns give the much sought-after Iberian ham.

BLUE-GREEN *leaves are densely covered with white hairs beneath; flowers are borne in drooping catkins.*

broadly
spreading
habit

leaf to
6cm long

HEIGHT *15m.* **SPREAD** *15m.*
BARK *Dark grey with small squarish plates.*
FLOWERING TIME *Late spring.*
OCCURRENCE *Plains and hills of Spain, Portugal, and S. France.*
SIMILAR SPECIES *Holm Oak (p.137), which has smaller, bitter acorns; Cork Oak (right), which has corky bark.*

Red Oak

Quercus rubra (Fagaceae)

This is a deciduous, spreading tree with smooth reddish shoots. Blue-green beneath, matt, dark green above, the alternate leaves are shallowly cut into bristle-tipped lobes and have stalks that are red at the base. The flowers are borne in catkins, the males yellow-green and pendulous, the females inconspicuous. Ripening the second year, only the base of the 3cm-long acorn is enclosed in a shallow cup.

DESPITE *the tree's name, the leaves often colour yellow or brown in autumn.*

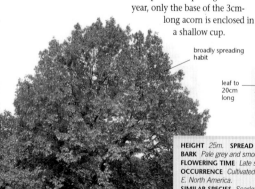

broadly spreading
habit

leaf to
20cm
long

HEIGHT *25m.* **SPREAD** *20m.*
BARK *Pale grey and smooth; later fissured.*
FLOWERING TIME *Late spring.*
OCCURRENCE *Cultivated; native to E. North America.*
SIMILAR SPECIES *Scarlet Oak (p.135) and Pin Oak (p.138), both of which have leaves that are glossy green below.*

Cork Oak

Quercus suber (Fagaceae)

The twigs of this evergreen, spreading tree often droop at the tips. The alternate, blue-green, oval leaves are wavy-edged with few shallow teeth at the margin and are covered beneath with white hairs. The flowers are borne in catkins, the males yellow-green and drooping, the females inconspicuous. Acorns ripen the first year, or the second year on some trees which may flower in autumn.

CORKY, *with prominent ridges, the bark is cut from the tree to make the corks for wine bottles and other items.*

broadly spreading habit

leaf to 7cm long

acorn to 3cm long

HEIGHT *20m.* **SPREAD** *20m.*
BARK *Pale grey, thick and corky.*
FLOWERING TIME *Late spring.*
OCCURRENCE *Woods; in W. Mediterranean often grown for cork production.*
SIMILAR SPECIES Holm Oak (p.137) and *Quercus rotundifolia (left), both of which lack the corky bark.*

Macedonian Oak

Quercus trojana (Fagaceae)

Upright when young, this deciduous or semi-evergreen, spreading tree retains its short-stalked, alternate leaves until late in the year. Male and female flowers are borne in separate catkins, the males yellow-green and drooping, the females inconspicuous. Acorns up to 3cm long are borne in a cup edged with bristly scales; and ripen the second year.

OVAL *to oblong, the glossy, green to grey-green leaves have up to 12 small, pointed teeth.*

spreading habit

leaf to 8cm long

HEIGHT *20m.*
SPREAD *15m.*
BARK *Grey-brown, growing fissured on older trees.*
FLOWERING TIME *Late spring.*
OCCURRENCE *Woods of S.E. Italy, the Balkans, and W. Turkey.*
SIMILAR SPECIES *None.*

Black Oak

Quercus velutina (Fagaceae)

DARK *grey and smooth, the bark becomes fissured with age, revealing orange inner bark.*

The young shoots and winter buds of this deciduous tree are covered with brown hairs, as is the underside of young leaves. Oval to elliptic, the alternate leaves are glossy, dark green and smooth, with bristle-tipped lobes. Flowers are borne in clusters, males yellow-green and pendulous, females inconspicuous. The acorns ripen in the second year.

broadly spreading habit

5–7 lobes

leaf to 30cm long

acorn to 2.5cm long

HEIGHT *25m.*
SPREAD *20m.*
BARK *Dark grey, smooth; fissured with age.*
FLOWERING TIME *Late spring.*
OCCURRENCE *Cultivated; native to E. North America.*
SIMILAR SPECIES *Red Oak (p.142), which has blue-green leaf undersides.*

Sweet Gum

Liquidambar styraciflua (Hamamelidaceae)

TOOTHED, *five-lobed, long-stalked leaves are often mistaken for those of a maple.*

The branches of this conical, deciduous tree often have corky ridges. The alternate, toothed leaves are glossy green above and turn yellow to orange, red, and purple in autumn. Tiny yellow-green male and female flowers open in separate, rounded clusters. The fruit, in rounded clusters 3cm wide, are edged with rough points. Many garden forms are popular for their autumn colour.

conical habit

leaf to 15cm long

HEIGHT *25m.* **SPREAD** *15m.*
BARK *Grey and smooth, becoming fissured and scaly with age.*
FLOWERING TIME *Late spring.*
OCCURRENCE *Cultivated; native to E. North America, Mexico, and Central America.*
SIMILAR SPECIES *Maples (Acer), which have opposite, rather than alternate, leaves.*

Persian Ironwood

Parrotia persica (Hamamelidaceae)

Usually branching low down, this deciduous, spreading tree has alternate, wavy-edged leaves, broadest towards the tip and shallowly toothed above the middle. Often with bronze-red margins when young, they are glossy green above and turn yellow, orange, red, and purple in autumn. The clusters of tiny, petalless flowers are made conspicuous by red anthers; they are followed by small brown fruit up to 8mm long.

FLAKING *bark with pale yellow-brown patches is an ornamental feature of this tree.*

leaf to 12cm long

broadly spreading habit

HEIGHT *15m.*
SPREAD *15m.*
BARK *Grey-brown, flaking in older trees.*
FLOWERING TIME *Late winter.*
OCCURRENCE *Cultivated; native to the Caucasus and N. Iran.*
SIMILAR SPECIES *None – a very distinct tree in its bark, leaves, and flowers.*

Laurus azorica

Laurus azorica (Lauraceae)

This evergreen, conical tree is similar to the much more widely distributed Bay Laurel (p.146). The alternate, broadly oval, leathery, dark green leaves are hairy beneath when young and are very aromatic when crushed. The small, greenish yellow flowers, about 1cm wide, are borne in clusters in the leaf axils, males and females on separate plants. The male flowers, with numerous stamens, are more noticeable. Female plants bear glossy black fruit up to 1.5cm long.

SMOOTH *and grey-brown, the bark is slightly roughened with small lenticels.*

conical habit

HEIGHT *20m.*
SPREAD *10m.*
BARK *Smooth and dark grey.*
FLOWERING TIME *Late spring.*
OCCURRENCE *Cultivated; native to the Azores and Canary Islands.*
SIMILAR SPECIES *Bay Laurel (p.146), which has smaller leaves and smooth shoots.*

leaf to 12cm long

Bay Laurel

Laurus nobilis (Lauraceae)

SMALL *greenish yellow flowers, 1cm wide, are borne in clusters from the leaf axils.*

This evergreen, conical tree is often shrubby, with many shoots arising from the base. The alternate, smooth, dark green, oval to oblong, aromatic leaves often have a wavy margin and taper gradually at the base. Male and female flowers are borne on separate plants. Female plants bear fleshy, berry-like fruit, which ripen from green to black. Also known as Sweet Bay, this is the laurel used as a herb in cooking.

conical habit

glossy green foliage

fruit to 1cm long

leaf to 10cm long

HEIGHT *20m.*
SPREAD *10m.*
BARK *Dark grey and smooth.*
FLOWERING TIME *Spring.*
OCCURRENCE *Woods in the Mediterranean region; commonly cultivated.*
SIMILAR SPECIES *Laurus azorica (p.145), which has larger leaves and hairy shoots.*

Redbud

Cercis canadensis (Leguminosae/Fabaceae)

PEA-LIKE *purple-pink flowers are borne in clusters on bare shoots before the leaves.*

Usually low-branching and often shrubby, the Redbud is a deciduous, spreading tree. The alternate, rounded leaves have a heart-shaped base and a short point at the tip. They are bronze when young, becoming dark green, and may turn yellow in autumn. Small and slender-stalked, the flowers are about 1cm long, and the fruit is a flat pod, 8cm long.

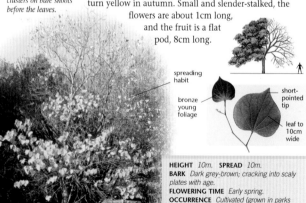

spreading habit

bronze young foliage

short-pointed tip

leaf to 10cm wide

HEIGHT *10m.* **SPREAD** *10m.*
BARK *Dark grey-brown; cracking into scaly plates with age.*
FLOWERING TIME *Early spring.*
OCCURRENCE *Cultivated (grown in parks and gardens); native to E. North America.*
SIMILAR SPECIES *Judas Tree (right) has blue-green leaves and larger flowers.*

Judas Tree

Cercis siliquastrum (Leguminosae/Fabaceae)

This deciduous, spreading tree has several main stems bearing alternate, rounded leaves, sometimes with a short-pointed tip. The leaves are blue-green above, paler beneath, and smooth on both sides. Flowers can form large clusters on the main trunks, and the fruit is a hanging, flattened pod, which ripens from green to pink and brown.

spreading habit

PINK *pea-like flowers, up to 2cm long, open in large, dense clusters, before and with the leaves.*

fruit to 10cm long

heart-shaped base

HEIGHT *10m.* **SPREAD** *10m.*
BARK *Grey-brown; cracking into small square plates with age.*
FLOWERING TIME *Spring.*
OCCURRENCE *Dry, rocky slopes in the E. Mediterranean region.*
SIMILAR SPECIES *Redbud (left) has dark green leaves and smaller flowers.*

Mount Etna Broom

Genista aetnensis (Leguminosae/Fabaceae)

A deciduous, spreading tree, or sometimes a shrub, this broom has slender, drooping green shoots. Small and narrow, the alternate leaves are few and rather inconspicuous and most have fallen by flowering time. The fruit is a dark brown pod, 1cm long, ending in a small point.

BRIGHT *golden yellow and pea-like, the fragrant flowers are borne singly along new shoots.*

spreading habit

leaf to 1cm long

HEIGHT *10m.*
SPREAD *10m.*
BARK *Grey-brown, deeply fissured at the base.*
FLOWERING TIME *Mid- to late summer.*
OCCURRENCE *Dry, rocky slopes in Sardinia and Sicily.*
SIMILAR SPECIES *None.*

Tulip Tree

Liriodendron tulipifera (Magnoliaceae)

CUP-SHAPED flowers, which open singly at the ends of the shoots, are green with orange bands.

Also known as Yellow Poplar, this fast-growing, large, deciduous tree has a broadly columnar head and green young shoots which are smooth or nearly so. The alternate leaves have four pointed lobes and are distinctively notched at the tip. They are glossy, dark green above and blue-green beneath, turning orange and yellow in autumn. The flowers have nine tepals, of which the outer three spread horizontally. The conical, pale brown fruit clusters are composed of many seeds with papery wings, often persisting over winter. 'Aureomarginatum' is a garden selection with yellow-edged leaves.

broadly columnar habit

NOTE

This tree produces a very fine timber which is popular in the manufacture of furniture and other wooden items.

leaf to 15cm long

flower 6cm wide

fruit to 6cm long

HEIGHT *30m.*
SPREAD *20m.*
BARK *Grey-brown, becoming deeply furrowed with age.*
FLOWERING TIME *Early summer.*
OCCURRENCE *Cultivated; native to E. North America.*
SIMILAR SPECIES *Chinese Tulip Tree (L. chinense), which is much more rarely seen and has more deeply cut leaves.*

Cucumber Tree

Magnolia acuminata (Magnoliaceae)

This vigorous, deciduous tree has a broadly conical head and stout shoots. Its alternate, large, oval leaves are untoothed and end in a short point. They are mid- to dark green above, paler and hairy beneath. The small flowers have nine tepals and are blue-green to yellow-green. The cylindrical, cucumber-shaped fruit ripen from green to pink then deep red.

CUP-SHAPED *flowers, up to 9cm long, are borne singly among the leaves at the ends of the shoots.*

broadly conical habit

leaf to 25cm long

fruit to 7cm long

HEIGHT *30m.*
SPREAD *20m.*
BARK *Grey-brown, with scaly ridges.*
FLOWERING TIME *Early summer.*
OCCURRENCE *Cultivated; native to E. North America.*
SIMILAR SPECIES *None – its small flowers make it distinct among magnolias.*

Campbell's Magnolia

Magnolia campbellii (Magnoliaceae)

A deciduous tree with a broadly conical head and stout, very smooth blue-green shoots, this magnolia has alternate, oval, short-pointed, untoothed leaves. Bronze when young, they turn dark green above, and paler or blue-green beneath. The flowers, with 16 tepals, emerge from silky hairy buds before the leaves and are followed by cylindrical red fruit clusters up to 15cm long.

SHOWY *flowers, up to 30cm wide, which open singly at the ends of the shoots, are produced in shades of pink to white, and are slightly fragrant.*

conical habit

leaf to 25cm or more

HEIGHT *20m.* **SPREAD** *15m.*
BARK *Grey and smooth.*
FLOWERING TIME *Late winter to early spring.*
OCCURRENCE *Cultivated; native to the Himalayas and S.W. China.*
SIMILAR SPECIES *None – its large size combined with its flowers make it distinct.*

Bull Bay

Magnolia grandiflora (Magnoliaceae)

CONE-LIKE *in appearance, the fruit is covered with green scales and brown hairs; red seeds emerge from it when ripe.*

The stout shoots of this conical, evergreen tree are covered in brown hairs. Its alternate, elliptic to oval, rigid, leathery, dark green leaves are paler beneath, sometimes covered with dark brown hairs. Large, fragrant, creamy white flowers open singly at the ends of shoots. Garden selections such as the hardy 'Exmouth' and the large-flowered 'Goliath' are grown.

glossy, dark green foliage

leaf to 25cm long

flower to 30cm wide

HEIGHT *15m.*
SPREAD *10m.*
BARK *Dark grey, smooth; developing scales on old trees.*
FLOWERING TIME *Summer.*
OCCURRENCE *Cultivated; native to S.E. USA.*
SIMILAR SPECIES *None – a very distinct tree as it is the only common evergreen magnolia.*

Magnolia kobus

Magnolia kobus (Magnoliaceae)

DARK *green leaves are paler and slightly hairy below; buds are covered in silky, grey hairs.*

The young shoots of this conical, deciduous tree exude a fragrance when scratched. Its alternate leaves are broadest above the middle, tapering to the base. The slightly fragrant, creamy white or pinkish flowers are held horizontally and have six large tepals with three smaller tepals at the base, opening before the leaves. The fruit is a cylindrical red cluster to 10cm long.

leaf to 15cm long

white flowers on bare branches

flower to 10cm wide

broadly conical habit

HEIGHT *12m.* **SPREAD** *15m.*
BARK *Grey and smooth.*
FLOWERING TIME *Early spring.*
OCCURRENCE *Cultivated; native to Japan and South Korea.*
SIMILAR SPECIES *Magnolia x loebneri, whose flowers have more tepals, which may be white or pink.*

Magnolia obovata

Magnolia obovata (Magnoliaceae)

The large, deep green leaves of this deciduous tree are widest above the middle, and are arranged in whorls at the tip of the shoots. The strongly fragrant flowers, each with 9–11 thick tepals, are creamy white with bright red stigmas. Cylindrical, spiky fruit, up to 20cm long, ripen to bright red.

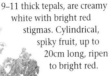

CUP-SHAPED *flowers are set in a whorl of leaves at the end of the shoots.*

leaf to 45cm long

broadly conical habit

flower 20cm wide

HEIGHT *15m.* **SPREAD** *12m.*
BARK *Grey and smooth.*
FLOWERING TIME *Early summer.*
OCCURRENCE *Cultivated; native to Japan.*
SIMILAR SPECIES *Only some infrequently seen species are similar such as M. macrophylla, M. officinalis, and M. x. wieseneri.*

Magnolia x soulangeana

Magnolia x soulangeana (Magnoliaceae)

A garden-raised hybrid between *Magnolia denudata* and *M. liliiflora*, this is a spreading, deciduous tree or large shrub, grown in many forms. The alternate, dark green leaves are widest towards the tip and end in a short point. The flowers have nine creamy white tepals, flushed with pink; the fruit appears in a cylindrical cluster and ripens from green to pink.

GOBLET-SHAPED *flowers are variable in colour, from creamy white to pink or purple-pink.*

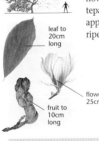

leaf to 20cm long

broadly spreading habit

flower to 25cm wide

fruit to 10cm long

HEIGHT *10m.* **SPREAD** *10m.*
BARK *Grey and smooth.*
FLOWERING TIME *Spring and early summer.*
OCCURRENCE *Known only in cultivation (grown in parks and gardens).*
SIMILAR SPECIES *None – the profuse, large pink and white flowers, and semi-shrubby habit, make it easily recognizable.*

Paper Mulberry

Broussonetia papyrifera (Moraceae)

This spreading, deciduous tree has bristly shoots and oval leaves, with a toothed margin, which may be deeply lobed or unlobed. Often purple-tinged when young, they become dark green as they mature. Male and female flowers are found on separate plants, with the white male flowers in cylindrical catkins and the green females in rounded heads with purple stigmas. The edible, spherical fruit clusters are up to 2cm wide.

DARK GREEN *leaves are roughly hairy above and covered with soft, grey hairs below.*

spreading habit

leaf to 20cm long

male catkin to 8cm wide

HEIGHT *15m.* **SPREAD** *15m.*
BARK *Grey-brown with shallow fissures.*
FLOWERING TIME *Spring or early summer.*
OCCURRENCE *Cultivated; naturalized in warm areas of Europe; native to China and Japan.*
SIMILAR SPECIES *White and Black Mulberries (right), which have oblong and not spherical fruit.*

Fig

Ficus carica (Moraceae)

Spreading and deciduous, this tree often branches low down, or is shrubby with stout green shoots. The deeply lobed leaves are glossy, dark green above and slightly rough with hairs. Tiny flowers, males and females on separate plants, are borne on the inside of the green structure that becomes the fruit. Familiar and edible, the figs ripen in autumn.

EACH *green, unripe fruit has a fleshy receptacle containing numerous small seeds; this ripens to a brown or purple, edible fig.*

spreading habit

leaf to 30cm long

purple, ripe fig

low branches

HEIGHT *10m.* **SPREAD** *10m.*
BARK *Grey and smooth.*
FLOWERING TIME *Early spring.*
OCCURRENCE *Cultivated; widely naturalized in the Mediterranean region; native to S.W. Asia.*
SIMILAR SPECIES *None – its leaf shape and unique fruit make it highly distinctive.*

White Mulberry

Morus alba (Moraceae)

Spreading and deciduous, this tree has very variable leaves that are smooth and glossy, dark green above, toothed, and may be unlobed or deeply lobed. Tiny green flowers are borne in short clusters about 1cm long, with the male and female flowers on the same or separate plants. The clustered, edible, distinctly stalked fruit may be white, pink, or red in colour.

OVAL to rounded, glossy green leaves, heart-shaped at the base, turn yellow in autumn.

spreading habit

leaf to 20cm long

fruit 2.5cm long

HEIGHT *15m.* **SPREAD** *15m.*
BARK *Orange-brown; fissured with age.*
FLOWERING TIME *Early summer.*
OCCURRENCE *Cultivated (particularly in warm areas); native to N. China.*
SIMILAR SPECIES *Paper Mulberry (left); Black Mulberry (below), which has rough leaves and unstalked fruit clusters.*

Black Mulberry

Morus nigra (Moraceae)

This deciduous, spreading tree often has a gnarled and irregular appearance. The oval leaves are toothed at the margin, with a heart-shaped base, and are often lobed. They are deep green, and roughly hairy above. Male and female flowers are tiny and green, and borne in short clusters, about 1cm long, on the same or separate plants.

EDIBLE *fruit clusters are deep red when ripe and generally unstalked.*

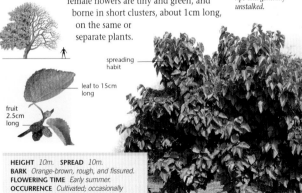

spreading habit

leaf to 15cm long

fruit 2.5cm long

HEIGHT *10m.* **SPREAD** *10m.*
BARK *Orange-brown, rough, and fissured.*
FLOWERING TIME *Early summer.*
OCCURRENCE *Cultivated; occasionally naturalized in S. Europe; native to Far East.*
SIMILAR SPECIES *Paper Mulberry (left); White Mulberry (above), which has smooth, glossy leaves, and stalked fruit clusters.*

Red Gum

Eucalyptus camaldulensis (Myrtaceae)

SMALL, *short-stalked flowers with numerous long white stamens are borne in clusters in the leaf axils.*

An evergreen tree, the Red Gum is broadly columnar or sometimes spreading. The slender, curved, alternate leaves are blue-green to grey-green on both sides and pendulous; young seedlings have bluish foliage. The flowers are borne in clusters, followed by small, woody, hemispherical fruit.

leaf to 20cm long

flower cluster to 5cm long

columnar to spreading habit

HEIGHT *40m or more.* **SPREAD** *25m.*
BARK *Grey-brown and creamy white, peeling in large flakes.*
FLOWERING TIME *Summer.*
OCCURRENCE *Cultivated in S. Europe; native to Australia.*
SIMILAR SPECIES *Blue Gum (below), which has large fruit borne singly.*

Blue Gum

Eucalyptus globulus (Myrtaceae)

LARGE, *woody, and prominently ribbed fruit, up to 3cm wide, follow the flowers.*

A vigorous, large, evergreen tree, the Blue Gum has a broadly columnar head. The slender, alternate, curved, and drooping leaves are blue-green; young plants have stalkless, silvery blue leaves. The white flowers have numerous stamens. They open singly in the axils of the leaves and are followed by the woody fruit.

columnar head

leaf to 30cm long

flower with numerous stamens

HEIGHT *40m.* **SPREAD** *25m.*
BARK *Grey-brown, pale brown, and creamy white, peeling in large flakes.*
FLOWERING TIME *Summer.*
OCCURRENCE *Cultivated in S. Europe; native to Tasmania and S.E. Australia.*
SIMILAR SPECIES *Although similar to other gums, it is recognized by its distinctive fruit.*

Cider Gum

Eucalyptus gunnii (Myrtaceae)

The aromatic, alternate, lance-shaped leaves on this evergreen tree are silvery at first, becoming blue-green. Leaves on young plants or from cut stumps are silvery blue and rounded. White flowers with numerous stamens are borne in clusters of three in the axils of the leaves, opening from silvery blue buds. The small, cup-shaped, woody fruit are 5mm long.

ROUGH *at the very base, the bark is grey, green, or orange, peeling in large patches, creamy when exposed.*

leaf to 10cm long

broadly columnar habit

HEIGHT *25m.* **SPREAD** *15m.*
BARK *Grey-brown and creamy white.*
FLOWERING TIME *Summer.*
OCCURRENCE *Cultivated; native to Tasmania and S.E. Australia.*
SIMILAR SPECIES *Several other gum trees, but none are as common in cool temperate regions.*

Ribbon Gum

Eucalyptus viminalis (Myrtaceae)

This evergreen tree with a broadly columnar head has red young shoots. The slender, alternate, long-pointed, and sometimes wavy-edged leaves are pale green. On young plants, they are dark green, ending in a point. Small white flowers with numerous stamens open in clusters of three in the axils of the leaves. They are followed by round, nearly stalkless fruit, about 6mm long.

GREY-BROWN *bark peels in large flakes to expose creamy white inner trunk.*

leaf to 18cm long

broadly columnar habit

HEIGHT *40m.* **SPREAD** *25m.*
BARK *Grey-brown and creamy white, peeling in large flakes; rough at the base.*
FLOWERING TIME *Summer.*
OCCURRENCE *Cultivated; native to Tasmania and S.E. Australia.*
SIMILAR SPECIES *Mountain Gum (E. dalrym-pleana), which has rounded juvenile leaves.*

Tree Privet

Ligustrum lucidum (Oleaceae)

SMALL, *fragrant white flowers hang from the ends of the shoots in large, conical clusters up to 20cm long.*

Conical when young, this evergreen tree spreads with age. The opposite, leathery leaves are oval, ending in a tapered point. Bronze when young, they mature to glossy, dark green. The flowers are followed by rounded blue-black fruit, up to 1cm long. Some variegated forms are also grown.

conical to spreading habit

leaf to 10cm long

HEIGHT *15m.*
SPREAD *15m.*
BARK *Grey and smooth.*
FLOWERING TIME *Summer.*
OCCURRENCE *Cultivated; native to China.*
SIMILAR SPECIES *Japanese Privet (L. japonicum), which is rarely grown, is smaller and shrubby with very thick leaves.*

Olive

Olea europaea (Oleaceae)

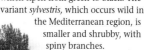

FRAGRANT, *tiny white, four-toothed flowers are borne in clusters in the leaf axils.*

Evergreen, round-headed, and with grey-white shoots, this tree often branches low down and is shrubby. The opposite untoothed leaves are grey-green above, grey-white beneath. Flower clusters are followed by the familiar olives which ripen from green to black. The variant *sylvestris,* which occurs wild in the Mediterranean region, is smaller and shrubby, with spiny branches.

round head

fruit to 4cm long

low branches

leaf to 8cm long

HEIGHT *15m; often kept low by pruning.*
SPREAD *10m.*
BARK *Pale grey and ridged.*
FLOWERING TIME *Summer.*
OCCURRENCE *Cultivated throughout the Mediterranean for fruit and oil, occasionally also ornamental; native to S.W. Asia.*
SIMILAR SPECIES *None.*

Phillyrea latifolia

Phillyrea latifolia (Oleaceae)

This evergreen, rounded, broadly spreading tree is upright when young with slender but rigid shoots. The opposite leaves are oval to lance-shaped, glossy, very dark green above, and with finely toothed or untoothed margins. On young plants, the leaves are larger and sharply toothed. Clusters of small, four-lobed, greenish white flowers open in the axils of the leaves.

ROUNDED *blue-black fruit, up to 1cm long, open after the flowers, in the axils of the leaves.*

dense foliage forms domed head

greenish white flower clusters

leaf to 6cm long

HEIGHT *10m.* **SPREAD** *10m.*
BARK *Dark grey; cracking into small squares.*
FLOWERING TIME *Early summer.*
OCCURRENCE *Evergreen woodland in dry areas of the Mediterranean.*
SIMILAR SPECIES *Strawberry Tree (p.128), which has superficially similar glossy foliage at a distance and has alternate leaves.*

Lilac

Syringa vulgaris (Oleaceae)

The Lilac is a deciduous, upright, tree-like shrub, which spreads with age. Oval or slightly heart-shaped, the opposite leaves have an untoothed margin and a pointed tip. The four-lobed flowers are borne in opposite pairs on the shoots. Small, brown, and oblong, the fruit is a taper-pointed capsule about 1cm long.

SMALL, *lilac flowers are tubular and fragrant and borne in dense clusters.*

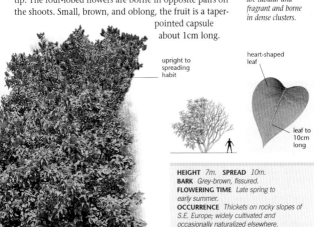

upright to spreading habit

heart-shaped leaf

leaf to 10cm long

HEIGHT *7m.* **SPREAD** *10m.*
BARK *Grey-brown, fissured.*
FLOWERING TIME *Late spring to early summer.*
OCCURRENCE *Thickets on rocky slopes of S.E. Europe; widely cultivated and occasionally naturalized elsewhere.*
SIMILAR SPECIES *None.*

Pittosporum tenuifolium

Pittosporum tenuifolium (Pittosporaceae)

The alternate leaves of this evergreen tree are produced on deep purple-black shoots. The small, tubular flowers, which open in the axils of the leaves, have a whitish base and five deep red-purple lobes and are very fragrant in the evening. Males and females are often borne on separate plants and may be either solitary or in clusters, the males having prominent yellow anthers. The fruit is a rounded, nearly black capsule about 1.2cm wide, which opens to reveal sticky seeds.

UNTOOTHED, *glossy, rather light green leaves are smooth, oblong, and with a wavy margin.*

broadly columnar head

flower about 1cm long

leaf 6cm long

HEIGHT *10m.*
SPREAD *6m.*
BARK *Dark grey and smooth.*
FLOWERING TIME *Late spring.*
OCCURRENCE *Cultivated in parks and gardens; native to New Zealand.*
SIMILAR SPECIES *None – this evergreen tree is easily recognized by the wavy-edged, glossy green leaves.*

NOTE

Several forms of this species are grown in gardens, including 'Purpureum' with purple foliage, and many variegated selections.

London Plane

Platanus x *hispanica* (Platanaceae)

This vigorous, large, deciduous tree with a spreading to broadly columnar head has alternate, maple-like leaves with five toothed lobes. Glossy bright green above, the leaves are paler beneath, with brown hairs when young. Tiny flowers are borne in pendulous, rounded clusters; male clusters yellow, females red. Dense, rounded fruit clusters persist on the tree over winter, in groups of up to six.

GREY, *brown, and cream, the bark begins to flake conspicuously in large patches with age.*

broadly columnar

leaf to 20cm long

HEIGHT *35m.* **SPREAD** *25m.*
BARK *Grey, brown, and cream.*
FLOWERING TIME *Late spring.*
OCCURRENCE *Known only in cultivation, a hybrid between the American Sycamore and Oriental Plane (below).*
SIMILAR SPECIES *Oriental Plane (below), which has more deeply lobed leaves.*

Oriental Plane

Platanus orientalis (Platanaceae)

A large, deciduous tree, this plane has a broadly columnar or spreading head of branches, the lower ones often drooping. The alternate, deeply lobed, maple-like leaves are glossy, deep green above and paler beneath, with brownish hairs when young. The tiny flowers are borne in pendulous, rounded heads. The males are yellow, the females red and followed by spherical fruit that persist on the tree in clusters.

OFTEN *found growing by water; this tree is frequently associated with willows, alders, poplars, and walnuts.*

leaf to 20cm long

fruit cluster 2.5cm wide

spreading habit

HEIGHT *30m.* **SPREAD** *25m.*
BARK *Grey-brown, pale brown, and creamy, flaking in large patches.*
FLOWERING TIME *Late spring.*
OCCURRENCE *River banks and mountain woods of S.E. Europe.*
SIMILAR SPECIES *London Plane (above), which has more shallowly lobed leaves.*

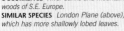

Pomegranate

Punica granatum (Punicaceae)

The Pomegranate is a deciduous, spreading tree, often branching low, or it may be shrub-like, with several upright, sometimes spiny, branches from the base. The opposite, oblong leaves are untoothed and emerge bronzy red, maturing to glossy, deep green. The showy flowers are followed by the familiar reddish to yellowish edible fruit.

FUNNEL-SHAPED *red flowers with crinkled petals open singly or in pairs at the ends of the shoots.*

flower to 4cm wide

leaf to 8cm long

fruit to 8cm wide

spreading habit

HEIGHT *8m.*
SPREAD *6m.*
BARK *Grey-brown, flaking.*
FLOWERING TIME *Summer.*
OCCURRENCE *Cultivated for its fruit and as an ornamental tree; naturalized in the Mediterranean region; native to S.W. Asia.*
SIMILAR SPECIES *None.*

Buckthorn

Rhamnus cathartica (Rhamnaceae)

Deciduous, spreading, and often shrubby, this tree has slender, rigid shoots that are frequently spine-tipped. Its opposite, oval, glossy green leaves have a finely toothed margin and turn yellow in autumn. Tiny, fragrant flowers are followed by fleshy, round berries, which ripen from green to black.

CLUSTERS *of tiny, four-lobed green flowers are borne in the axils of the leaves.*

spreading habit

leaf to 6cm long

dense fruit clusters

HEIGHT *5m.*
SPREAD *6m.*
BARK *Orange-brown, scaly.*
FLOWERING TIME *Summer.*
OCCURRENCE *Woods, thickets, and hedgerows of Europe; often on chalky soils.*
SIMILAR SPECIES *Alder Buckthorn (right), which has untoothed, alternate leaves.*

Alder Buckthorn

Rhamnus frangula (Rhamnaceae)

This is a deciduous, spreading or shrubby tree, often with several main stems. The alternate, untoothed leaves are widest towards the end, where there is a short point. They are glossy, dark green above, paler beneath, and turn yellow or red in autumn. The fleshy, rounded fruit are green becoming red and then ripening to black.

TINY *flowers are green tinged with pink and borne in dense clusters in the leaf axils.*

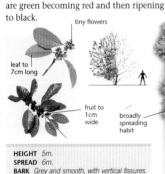

tiny flowers

leaf to 7cm long

fruit to 1cm wide

broadly spreading habit

HEIGHT *5m.*
SPREAD *6m.*
BARK *Grey and smooth, with vertical fissures.*
FLOWERING TIME *Summer.*
OCCURRENCE *Woods, thickets, and hedgerows of Europe; often on wet soil.*
SIMILAR SPECIES *Buckthorn (left), which has opposite leaves and whose fruit are never red.*

Snowy Mespilus

Amelanchier lamarckii (Rosaceae)

Often shrubby, this deciduous, spreading tree usually has several stems starting from the base. The oval, pointed, alternate leaves have a finely toothed margin. Bronze and covered in silky hairs when young, they mature to dark green and turn red in autumn. The white flowers are borne in clusters opening with the young foliage and have five slender petals.

ROUNDED *and purple-black, the fruit are up to 1cm wide and very juicy.*

red autumn foliage

leaf to 8cm long

5-petalled flowers

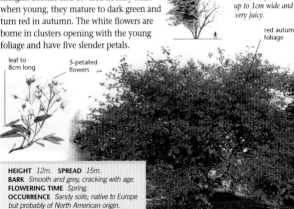

HEIGHT *12m.* **SPREAD** *15m.*
BARK *Smooth and grey, cracking with age.*
FLOWERING TIME *Spring.*
OCCURRENCE *Sandy soils; native to Europe but probably of North American origin.*
SIMILAR SPECIES *Can be confused only with rarer Amelanchier species seen in gardens.*

Azarole

Crataegus azarolus (Rosaceae)

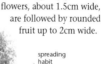

A spreading, deciduous tree, the Azarole has spiny shoots that are hairy when young. The alternate leaves are lobed, oval or diamond-shaped, and narrow at the base. Downy on both sides when young, they later become smooth and glossy green above. Clusters of white flowers, about 1.5cm wide, are followed by rounded fruit up to 2cm wide.

ROUNDED, *yellow to orange or red, edible fruit have an apple-like flavour.*

leaf 8cm long

narrow base

spreading habit

spiny shoot

HEIGHT 10m. **SPREAD** 10m.
BARK Grey-brown, growing fissured with age.
FLOWERING TIME Early summer.
OCCURRENCE Scrub and woodland margins on hill slopes; native to Crete; naturalized in S. Europe.
SIMILAR SPECIES Oriental Thorn (right), which has sharply toothed leaf lobes.

Cockspur Thorn

Crataegus crus-galli (Rosaceae)

Armed with sharp spines up to 8cm long, this deciduous tree has a spreading, often flattened head, and bears clusters of white flowers, each 1.5cm wide. The alternate, unlobed, dark green leaves are widest towards the rounded tip and narrow at the base, turning orange and red in autumn. The ripe fruit, up to 1cm wide, persist well into winter.

FLESHY *and edible, rounded red fruit hang in clusters from long, thin stalks.*

flattened head

spreading habit

leaves glossy above

leaf 10cm long

HEIGHT 8m.
SPREAD 10m.
BARK Dark grey-brown, scaly with age.
FLOWERING TIME Early summer.
OCCURRENCE Cultivated; native to E. North America.
SIMILAR SPECIES C. x persimilis, whose fruit fall soon after ripening.

fruit to 1cm wide

Oriental Thorn

Crataegus laciniata (Rosaceae)

The somewhat spiny shoots of this deciduous, spreading tree are white with hairs when young. The alternate leaves are diamond-shaped in outline and deeply cut into five or more sharply toothed lobes. They are glossy, dark green above and covered with grey hairs on the underside.

CLUSTERED *white flowers, up to 2cm wide, have pink anthers.*

The clusters of white flowers are followed by rounded to oblong, red or yellow-flushed fruit that are edible.

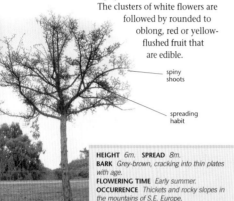

spiny shoots

spreading habit

leaf to 5cm long

fruit to 2cm long

HEIGHT *6m.* **SPREAD** *8m.*
BARK *Grey-brown, cracking into thin plates with age.*
FLOWERING TIME *Early summer.*
OCCURRENCE *Thickets and rocky slopes in the mountains of S.E. Europe.*
SIMILAR SPECIES *Azarole (left), which has bluntly lobed leaves.*

Midland Hawthorn

Crataegus laevigata (Rosaceae)

The alternate leaves of this deciduous, spreading tree are shallowly divided into blunt lobes and are usually broadest above the middle. They are glossy, dark green above and paler beneath. Shoots are smooth and glossy. Rounded to oval, inedible, bright red fruit, with two seeds, follow the white flowers. 'Paul's Scarlet' is a commonly planted hybrid with deep pink, double flowers.

WHITE *flowers, to 2cm wide, have red anthers, and are borne in small clusters.*

spreading habit

leaf to 5cm long

fruit to 2cm long

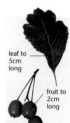

HEIGHT *10m.* **SPREAD** *10m.*
BARK *Grey and smooth, cracking with age.*
FLOWERING TIME *Late spring.*
OCCURRENCE *Woods, usually with clay soils, all over Europe.*
SIMILAR SPECIES *Hawthorn (p.165), which has more deeply lobed leaves and fruit with a single stone.*

Crataegus x lavalleei

Crataegus x *lavalleei* (Rosaceae)

ROUNDED *green fruit on short stalks are borne in clusters in autumn and ripen to reddish green.*

A hybrid species, this spreading tree has sparsely spiny shoots that are hairy when young. Its large, alternate leaves, widest above the middle, with a tapered base and short-pointed tip, remain on the tree well into winter. They are glossy, dark green above, but grey and hairy beneath. In early to midsummer, white flowers with pink anthers are borne in flattened clusters on hairy stalks, followed by rounded red fruit ripening in late autumn. The commonly grown form of this hybrid is known as 'Carrièrei'.

> **NOTE**
>
> This tree is a hybrid between Cockspur Thorn (C. crus-galli) *and* Crataegus mexicana. *It originated in France and has now become a popular street tree.*

glossy foliage

spreading habit

leaf to 10cm long

flower 2.5cm wide

fruit 2cm wide

HEIGHT *10m.*
SPREAD *12m.*
BARK *Dark grey, flaking in scaly plates.*
FLOWERING TIME *Summer.*
OCCURRENCE *Known only in cultivation (grown in parks, gardens, and streets).*
SIMILAR SPECIES *A very distinct tree easily recognizable by its dark green, semi-evergreen foliage and its late-ripening fruit.*

Hawthorn

Crataegus monogyna (Rosaceae)

The smooth, thorny shoots of this deciduous species are often somewhat pendulous on old trees. The alternate leaves are oval to diamond-shaped in outline, with a broadly tapered base. They are deeply cut into three or five sharply toothed lobes and are glossy, dark green above and paler beneath. The fragrant white flowers have pink anthers and are borne in dense clusters. These are followed by bright red oval fruit up to 1.2cm wide, each containing a single stone. The Hawthorn is a variable and widely distributed species, often used for hedging.

SHINY, *bright red fruit or hips ripen in attractive clusters at the end of branches from September to October.*

white blossom

broadly spreading habit

flower to 1.5cm wide

leaf to 5cm long

NOTE

The garden selection 'Biflora', known as the Glastonbury Thorn, flowers twice: once in winter or early spring, depending on the weather, and again at the normal time of late spring. It was said to have grown from the staff of Joseph of Arimathea, which he plunged into the ground at Glastonbury when he came to England from the Holy Land.

HEIGHT *10m.*
SPREAD *10m.*
BARK *Orange-brown; cracked and scaly in old trees.*
FLOWERING TIME *Late spring.*
OCCURRENCE *Woods, scrub, and hedgerows throughout Europe.*
SIMILAR SPECIES *Midland Hawthorn (p.163), which has less deeply cut leaves with three to five more or less blunt lobes and fruit containing two stones.*

Crataegus rhipidophylla

Crataegus rhipidophylla (Rosaceae)

DEEP *red fruit are longer than wide, up to 12mm long, and contain a single seed.*

This deciduous, spreading tree is sometimes shrubby and has smooth, often spiny shoots. The alternate, oval, dark green leaves are paler beneath and have sharply toothed lobes and toothed stipules at the base. The white flowers have numerous stamens with pink anthers and are borne in open clusters.

leaf to 7cm long

flower to 2cm wide

spreading habit

HEIGHT *8m.* **SPREAD** *8m.*
BARK *Grey-brown, scaly on old trees.*
FLOWERING TIME *Late spring.*
OCCURRENCE *Woods of Norway and Sweden.*
SIMILAR SPECIES *Whitebeam (p.191), which is a larger tree, has larger leaves, and may be naturalized in the same area.*

Loquat

Eriobotrya japonica (Rosaceae)

FLESHY, *edible orange-yellow fruit are up to 6cm long.*

Sometimes shrubby, this evergreen, spreading tree has stout, hairy shoots. The large, leathery, alternate leaves are toothed at the edge and broadest above the middle. They are glossy dark green above with prominent veins and densely hairy beneath. The fragrant white flowers open in conical clusters at the ends of the shoots and are followed by spherical to pear-shaped fruit.

flower to 1cm wide

glossy dark green canopy

leaf to 25cm long

HEIGHT *10m* **SPREAD** *10m.*
BARK *Grey-brown, grows fissured on older trees.*
FLOWERING TIME *Autumn.*
OCCURRENCE *Cultivated, particularly in the Mediterranean; native to China, occasionally naturalized in S. Europe.*
SIMILAR SPECIES *None.*

Quince

Cydonia oblonga (Rosaceae)

The young shoots of this deciduous, spreading tree are densely covered in white hairs, later becoming smooth. The alternate, untoothed, short-stalked leaves are oval to nearly rounded. They are hairy when young, becoming dark green and smooth above, densely covered in grey-white hairs beneath. The pear-shaped or apple-shaped, fragrant yellow fruit, which are covered in white woolly hairs when young, are used in preserves.

PALE *pink or white flowers, up to 5cm wide, have five petals and are borne singly.*

leaf to 10cm long

fruit to 10cm long

HEIGHT *8m.*
SPREAD *8m.*
BARK *Purple-brown and flaking.*
FLOWERING TIME *Late spring.*
OCCURRENCE *Widely cultivated; naturalized in the Mediterranean; native to C. and S.W. Asia.*
SIMILAR SPECIES *Common Pear (p.188), which has toothed leaves and fruit borne in clusters.*

NOTE

Several selections are grown for their fruit such as 'Luisitanica', with deep yellow fruit and 'Vranja', with golden-yellow, very fragrant fruit.

Cultivated Apple

Malus domestica (Rosaceae)

This deciduous, spreading tree with a rounded head and hairy young shoots is a hybrid, of which *Malus dasyphylla* is probably one of the parents. The alternate, oval leaves are dark green above and hairy beneath. Five-petalled flowers are followed by edible green, yellow, or red fruit.

WHITE *flowers flushed pink, 5cm wide, open in clusters from deep pink buds.*

broadly spreading habit

fruit to 10cm wide

leaf to 12cm long

HEIGHT *10m.*
SPREAD *10m.*
BARK *Grey- to purple-brown; flaking with age.*
FLOWERING TIME *Late spring.*
OCCURRENCE *Cultivated in gardens and orchards for its fruit; naturalized in Europe.*
SIMILAR SPECIES *M. dasyphylla, which has small yellow or red-flushed fruit.*

Malus florentina

Malus florentina (Rosaceae)

The alternate, broad, oval leaves of this deciduous tree have several toothed lobes on each side. They are deep green above, densely covered with white hairs beneath, and turn orange, red, and purple in autumn. Clustered white flowers are followed by small, rounded to pear-shaped fruit. The small sepals fall before the fruit ripens. This rare species may be a hybrid between a *Malus* and a *Sorbus*.

RED- *to purple-brown bark flakes in small, thin, square plates and turns orange-brown when exposed.*

broadly columnar habit

flowers 2cm wide

leaf to 6cm long

fruit 1cm wide

HEIGHT *8m.* **SPREAD** *6m.*
BARK *Red-brown to purple-brown, flaking.*
FLOWERING TIME *Late spring to early summer.*
OCCURRENCE *Woods, thickets, and rocky places; N. Italy to N. Greece.*
SIMILAR SPECIES *M. trilobata has larger, long-stalked leaves, and its sepals do not fall.*

Japanese Crab Apple

Malus x *floribunda* (Rosaceae)

There is a dense head of arching shoots on this small, deciduous, spreading tree. The alternate, narrowly oval, sharply toothed, taper-pointed leaves are dark green and can be lobed on vigorous shoots. They are smooth above and hairy beneath when young. Profusely borne, the flowers, 2.5cm wide, open as the leaves emerge and are followed by small, rounded fruit.

DEEP *red in bud, the five-petalled, clustered flowers open pale pink as the leaves emerge, and become almost white.*

leaf to 10cm long

arching shoots

fruit 8mm wide

HEIGHT *5m.*
SPREAD *6m.*
BARK *Purple-brown, flaking with age.*
FLOWERING TIME *Spring.*
OCCURRENCE *Cultivated in parks, gardens, and streets; a hybrid of Japanese origin.*
SIMILAR SPECIES *None – distinctive in its small size, dense habit, and profuse flowers.*

Malus hupehensis

Malus hupehensis (Rosaceae)

This vigorous, deciduous tree has a broad, rounded head. The alternate, oval, finely toothed leaves, to 10cm long, end in a tapered point and are dark green above when mature, turning yellow in autumn. Flowers with five broad, overlapping petals are followed by small, cherry-like, slightly flattened red fruit borne on slender stalks.

FRAGRANT *white flowers open profusely in large clusters from pink buds.*

broadly spreading habit

HEIGHT *12m.*
SPREAD *15m.*
BARK *Purple-brown, flaking on old trees.*
FLOWERING TIME *Spring.*
OCCURRENCE *Cultivated; native to China.*
SIMILAR SPECIES *None – its vigorous habit, white flowers, and small fruit make this tree distinctive.*

fruit to 1cm wide

flower to 5cm wide

Crab Apple hybrids

Malus hybrids (Rosaceae)

'EVERESTE' *is one of the many crab apples grown for their ornamental fruit.*

Numerous hybrids of crab apple species are raised in gardens, with a variety of flowers and fruit. They are spreading, deciduous trees with oval, dark green or purple leaves. The flowers vary from white to pink and may be single or semi-double. Popular forms include 'Golden Hornet', with pink-flushed, white flowers and deep yellow fruit; 'Profusion', with deep red-purple young leaves, and purple-red flowers followed by red-purple fruit; and 'Van Eseltine', with upright branches and double pink flowers.

spreading habit

leaf to 10 cm long | white blossom | deep yellow fruit
'GOLDEN HORNET'

purple-red blossom
'PROFUSION'

double flowers
'VAN ESELTINE'

HEIGHT *8m.*
SPREAD *10m.*
BARK *Grey-brown to purple-brown, flaking on old trees.*
FLOWERING TIME *Late spring to early summer.*
OCCURRENCE *Cultivated in parks, gardens, and streets.*
SIMILAR SPECIES *Many Malus hybrids are cultivated in gardens with flowers ranging from white to red and with small to large fruit of various colours. Some have purple leaves.*

NOTE

Crab Apple hybrids are grown in a wide range of forms as ornamental trees for their flowers and the fruit, that follow in autumn.

Wild Apple

Malus sylvestris (Rosaceae)

This deciduous, spreading tree or shrub sometimes has spiny shoots. The oval to nearly rounded leaves have finely toothed margins and short-pointed tips; they are dark green above, paler below, and smooth or nearly so on both sides when mature. White or pink-tinged flowers, to 4cm wide, are borne in clusters, followed by small, yellow-green or red-flushed fruit.

WHITE, *often pink-tinged flowers appear in clusters in April and May.*

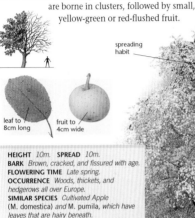

spreading habit

leaf to 8cm long

fruit to 4cm wide

HEIGHT *10m.* **SPREAD** *10m.*
BARK *Brown, cracked, and fissured with age.*
FLOWERING TIME *Late spring.*
OCCURRENCE *Woods, thickets, and hedgerows all over Europe.*
SIMILAR SPECIES *Cultivated Apple (M. domestica) and M. pumila, which have leaves that are hairy beneath.*

Malus trilobata

Malus trilobata (Rosaceae)

A deciduous and conical tree, sometimes a shrub, *Malus trilobata* has young shoots with white hairs and long-stalked, maple-like, dark green leaves, deeply cut into three lobes. In autumn, these turn yellow, red, and finally purple. The white flowers, at the end of the shoots, are followed by rounded green or red-flushed fruit, up to 3cm wide.

SMALL *and hard, the fruit, are often slightly wider than long, and have three persistent sepals.*

conical habit

leaf to 10cm long

flower 4cm wide

HEIGHT *15m.* **SPREAD** *6m.*
BARK *Grey-brown, cracking into small, square plates.*
FLOWERING TIME *Early summer.*
OCCURRENCE *Evergreen thickets of N.E. Greece.*
SIMILAR SPECIES *M. florentina, which has smaller leaves and fruit with no sepals.*

Medlar

Mespilus germanica (Rosaceae)

ROUNDED *but flat-topped, hard, brown fruit have persistent green sepals.*

A deciduous tree, sometimes with thorny shoots, the Medlar has alternate, oblong, dark green leaves that may be untoothed or have small teeth towards the tip. Its white flowers are borne singly, followed by pear-shaped to rounded, russet-brown fruit up to 3cm wide. Wild plants are more shrubby and spiny than those in cultivation, with smaller leaves, flowers, and fruit.

spreading habit

flower to 5cm wide

leaf to 15cm long

HEIGHT *6m.* **SPREAD** *8m.*
BARK *Grey-brown and orange-brown; cracking into thin plates with age.*
FLOWERING TIME *Late spring to early summer.*
OCCURRENCE *Woods and thickets in S.E. Europe; naturalized in C. Europe.*
SIMILAR SPECIES *None.*

Photinia davidiana

Photinia davidiana (Rosaceae)

TINY *bright red fruit hang from long stalks in small clusters, at the ends of the shoots.*

This evergreen tree often produces several stems from the base and is sometimes shrubby. Its alternate, oblong leaves are untoothed with a small, tapered point. Matt, dark green above, they are paler beneath, the older leaves turning red before they fall. Small white flowers open in dense clusters at the end of the shoots and are followed by rounded fruit up to 8mm wide.

flower 6mm wide

rounded head

leaf to 12cm long

HEIGHT *10m.* **SPREAD** *10m.*
BARK *Grey-brown and smooth.*
FLOWERING TIME *Summer.*
OCCURRENCE *Cultivated; native to China and Vietnam.*
SIMILAR SPECIES *P. x fraseri (right) and the less common P. serratifolia, which both have toothed leaves.*

Photinia x fraseri

Photinia x fraseri (Rosaceae)

Like its relative *Photinia davidiana* (left), this tree is evergreen and sometimes produces several stems from the base or has a shrubby habit. Its alternate leaves are broadest towards the tip; they are bronze-red when they first emerge, turning glossy, dark green later. The small white flowers with pink anthers open in flattened heads. They are followed by usually sparse, rounded red fruit, up to 5mm wide. This is a hybrid between *P. glabra* and *P. serratifolia;* two popular forms derived from it are 'Red Robin' and 'Robusta'.

OBLONG *leaves are toothed and smooth; the young foliage is bronze-red in colour.*

rounded head

broadly spreading habit

bronze-red young leaves

flowerhead to 10cm wide

leaf to 15cm long

finely toothed leaf margin

HEIGHT *10m.* **SPREAD** *8m.*
BARK *Grey-brown and smooth; peeling in flakes on old trees.*
FLOWERING TIME *Late spring and summer.*
OCCURRENCE *Known only in cultivation (grown in parks and gardens, and used as a container plant).*
SIMILAR SPECIES *P. davidiana (left), which has untoothed leaves; P. serratifolia, which is a larger tree with leaves to 20cm long and flowerheads to 15cm wide.*

NOTE

Photinia x fraseri was first developed as a hybrid in the USA. It is a popular tree among gardeners for its colourful young foliage.

Photinia villosa

Photinia villosa (Rosaceae)

OVAL, *bright red fruit, up to 1cm long, nestle among the bright red and orange autumn leaves.*

This deciduous, spreading tree is sometimes shrubby. The alternate leaves are oval or broadest towards the end, with a finely toothed margin and tapered point at the tip. Bronzy when young and usually hairy, they mature to dark green. Flattened clusters of small white flowers with pink anthers are followed by the fruit.

The stalks of both the flowers and fruit are rough with small warts.

spreading habit

small white flowers

leaf to 8cm long

HEIGHT *8m.* **SPREAD** *10m.*
BARK *Grey-brown, shallowly fissured.*
FLOWERING TIME *Late spring.*
OCCURRENCE *Cultivated; native to China, Japan, and Korea.*
SIMILAR SPECIES *None – distinct from all* Crataegus *species in the lack of thorns and warty flower and fruit stalks.*

Apricot

Prunus armeniaca (Rosaceae)

ORANGE-YELLOW, *often flushed with red, the rounded fruit is edible and sweet.*

The Apricot is a deciduous, spreading tree with smooth reddish shoots. The alternate, broadly oval to nearly round leaves have a finely toothed margin, ending abruptly in a short point. They open bronzy red and mature to glossy, dark green. Pale pink or white flowers, 2.5cm wide, open on the shoots before the leaves emerge.

The fruit are densely covered in short, soft hairs.

clusters of pink flowers

leaf to 10cm long

fruit to 4cm wide

HEIGHT *10m.*
SPREAD *10m.*
BARK *Smooth and red-brown.*
FLOWERING TIME *Early spring.*
OCCURRENCE *Cultivated and occasionally naturalized; native to N. China.*
SIMILAR SPECIES *Peach (p.183), has slender, long-pointed leaves and different fruit.*

Wild Cherry

Prunus avium (Rosaceae)

A deciduous tree, the Wild Cherry or Gean is conical when young becoming broadly columnar to spreading with age. Elliptic to oblong, the alternate, sharply toothed leaves are up to 15cm long and taper abruptly to a short point at the tip. They are bronze when young, maturing to matt, dark green, and turn yellow or red in autumn. Conspicuous glands can be seen at the top of leaf stalks. The rounded, slender-stalked cherries ripen to red and are edible. 'Plena' is a selection with double flowers, which is commonly planted in streets, parks, and gardens.

FIVE-PETALLED *white flowers, 3cm wide, are borne in clusters just before or as the young leaves emerge.*

profusion of white flowers

spreading habit

fruit to 1cm wide

flower to 3cm wide

pink-tinged buds

HEIGHT *25m.*
SPREAD *15m.*
BARK *Red-brown, smooth, and glossy at first; peeling horizontally in strips.*
FLOWERING TIME *Spring.*
OCCURRENCE *Woodlands of Europe.*
SIMILAR SPECIES *Sour Cherry (p.177), which is a smaller, often shrubby, tree with acid fruit and finely toothed leaves.*

NOTE

The tallest European cherry, this species has given rise to the sweet cherries that have sweet, edible red or black fruit. These are widely cultivated for their very popular fruit.

Cherry Plum

Prunus cerasifera (Rosaceae)

FIVE-PETALLED, *white flowers, 2.5cm wide, open singly or in clusters.*

A deciduous, thicket-forming shrub or a small, spreading tree, the Cherry Plum has hairy, sometimes spiny shoots. The alternate, oval, sharply toothed leaves are glossy, dark green and smooth above, downy on the veins beneath. White flowers open along the shoot before the leaves emerge. The rounded, plum-like red fruit, 3cm wide, are sweet and edible. Purple-leaved forms of this tree are commonly grown: *P. cerasifera* 'Nigra' has pink flowers, while *P. cerasifera* 'Pissardii' has white flowers.

broadly spreading habit

leaf to 6cm long

HEIGHT *8m.*
SPREAD *10m.*
BARK *Purple-brown, scaly, flaking with age.*
FLOWERING TIME *Early spring.*
OCCURRENCE *Naturalized in thickets and hedgerows; native origin uncertain.*
SIMILAR SPECIES *Blackthorn (p.185), which is more shrubby with blue-black, bitter fruit; it flowers several weeks later.*

NOTE

The purple-leaved forms of the Cherry Plum are popular trees, and are often seen planted in parks, gardens and streets.

Sour Cherry

Prunus cerasus (Rosaceae)

This small, spreading, deciduous tree is often shrubby, with suckers at the base and smooth shoots. The alternate, oval leaves are glossy, dark green above, smooth on both sides, and finely toothed with tapered points. The red or black fruit that follow the five-petalled flowers are sour but edible. *P. cerasus* 'Rhexii' is a garden selection grown for its double flowers; numerous other selections are grown for their edible fruit. 'Semperflorens' (All Saints' Cherry) continues to flower through summer.

LONG-STALKED *white flowers, with green sepals, are 2cm wide and open in small clusters before the leaves emerge.*

NOTE

This species is commonly grown for its fruit, which is the commercially grown Sour Cherry.

broadly spreading habit

leaf to 8cm long

fruit to 2cm wide

HEIGHT *8m.*
SPREAD *8m.*
BARK *Purple-brown, peeling in horizontal strips.*
FLOWERING TIME *Spring.*
OCCURRENCE *Cultivated in gardens and orchards; widely naturalized in Europe; origin uncertain.*
SIMILAR SPECIES *Wild Cherry (p.175), which is a larger tree with bigger leaves that are hairy beneath and sweet or bitter fruit.*

Prunus cocomilia

Prunus cocomilia (Rosaceae)

Sometimes shrubby, this spreading, deciduous tree has smooth, spineless shoots. The alternate, oval, dark green leaves have a toothed margin and are smooth on both sides. White flowers, about 1cm wide, open in small clusters of three to four along the shoots as the young leaves open. They are followed by edible plum-like fruit which have a single stone.

EDIBLE *yellow, sometimes red-flushed, fruit are oval and up to 4cm long.*

spreading habit

leaf to 4cm long

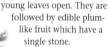

fissured, grey-brown bark

HEIGHT *6m.*
SPREAD *6m.*
BARK *Grey-brown, fissured on old plants.*
FLOWERING TIME *Spring.*
OCCURRENCE *Thickets and mountain slopes in S. Italy and the S. Balkans.*
SIMILAR SPECIES *Plum (below), which has hairy leaves and shoots.*

Plum

Prunus domestica (Rosaceae)

The Plum is a rounded to spreading, deciduous tree. It has spineless shoots that are hairy when young. The alternate, dark, matt green leaves are oval or widest towards the end and hairy beneath, with toothed margins. Small white flowers are borne singly or in clusters of up to three on the bare shoots before the leaves emerge. When ripe, the flesh of the edible fruit separates easily from the stone.

ROUNDED *to egg-shaped, the edible fruit is smooth-skinned, red, yellow, or purple, and up to 8cm long.*

white flowers line bare shoots

leaf to 8cm long

flower to 2.5cm wide

HEIGHT *10m.* **SPREAD** *10m.*
BARK *Grey-brown, fissured with age.*
FLOWERING TIME *Spring.*
OCCURRENCE *Cultivated (grown in gardens and orchards); widely naturalized in Europe.*
SIMILAR SPECIES *P. cocomilia (above), has smooth shoots and leaves; Bullace (right), flesh does not separate easily from the stone.*

Almond

Prunus dulcis (Rosaceae)

This deciduous, spreading tree has smooth, green or red-flushed shoots. The alternate, lance-shaped, glossy green leaves are smooth on both sides, with a toothed margin and long, tapered tip. The five-petalled flowers open before the leaves emerge. The green fruit is covered with velvety hairs; when ripe, the flesh separates from the flattened stone which contains an edible, white seed. Wild plants are spiny; cultivated plants are spineless.

PALE *pink or white flowers, up to 5cm wide, open on the bare shoots.*

leaf to 12cm long

fruit to 6cm long

profusion of pink to white flowers

HEIGHT *8m.* **SPREAD** *10m.*
BARK *Dark grey, later cracks into squares.*
FLOWERING TIME *Early spring.*
OCCURRENCE *Cultivated (for its fruit and as an ornamental); naturalized in S. Europe; native to S.W. and C. Asia, and N. Africa.*
SIMILAR SPECIES *Peach (p.183), which has fleshy fruit with a grooved stone.*

Bullace

Prunus insititia (Rosaceae)

The often spiny shoots of this deciduous, spreading tree are densely hairy when young. It has alternate, oval, bluntly-toothed, matt, dark green leaves that are hairy on both sides and abruptly short-pointed at the tip. Small white flowers open singly or in clusters of up to three, before or as the leaves emerge. The edible fruit has a rounded stone that clings to the flesh. Mirabelle plums and damsons are selected forms of Bullace.

ROUNDED *to egg-shaped, the edible fruit, up to 5cm long, is sweet and fleshy.*

broadly spreading habit

flower to 2.5cm wide

leaf to 8cm long

HEIGHT *7m.* **SPREAD** *10m.*
BARK *Dark grey and smooth; fissured on old trees.*
FLOWERING TIME *Spring.*
OCCURRENCE *Cultivated for its edible fruit; widely naturalized in Europe; of garden origin.*
SIMILAR SPECIES *Plum (left), has a flattened stone that separates easily from the flesh.*

Japanese Cherries

Prunus (Rosaceae)

DEEP pink, double flowers of 'Kanzan', the most popular and commonly planted Japanese cherry (also main picture).

These deciduous trees are cultivated *Prunus* forms or hybrids. They have alternate, sharply toothed dark green leaves, often bronze when young, usually ending in a long, tapered point. The showy flowers can be pink or white, single, semi-double, or double. Commonly seen forms are 'Amanogawa' with an upright habit and pale pink double flowers; 'Kanzan' is vase-shaped at first, branching later, with deep pink, double flowers; 'Shirotae' is wide spreading with drooping branches and large clusters of white single to semi-double flowers; 'Shôgetsu' has large, white double flowers; and 'Taihaku' has very large, single white flowers.

usually spreading habit

leaf to 15cm long

large double flowers

yellow anthers

'KANZAN'　　**'AMANOGAWA'**　　**'SHÔGETSU'**

HEIGHT *10m or more.*
SPREAD *15m or more.*
BARK *Red-brown with horizontal bands.*
FLOWERING TIME *Spring.*
OCCURRENCE *Known only in cultivation (grown in gardens, parks, and streets).*
SIMILAR SPECIES *P. avium 'Plena', which is a much larger tree; Sargent's Cherry (p.184), which has single flowers in unstalked clusters.*

NOTE

These ornamental garden trees are of ancient origin in Japan, where they have been cultivated for over a thousand years.

Cherry Laurel

Prunus laurocerasus (Rosaceae)

This evergreen, rounded tree is usually shrubby with stout, smooth shoots that are green when young. The alternate, leathery, oblong leaves are smooth on both sides with small teeth above the middle and end in a short point. The flowers are followed by rounded fruit which ripen from green to red, then glossy black. The Cherry Laurel is grown in many forms, often as low shrubs, varying in habit and leaf.

FRAGRANT *white flowers, each 8mm wide, are borne in cylindrical clusters in spring.*

spreading habit

leaf to 20cm long

flower cluster to 12cm long

fruit to 1.5cm wide

HEIGHT *10m.*
SPREAD *10m.*
BARK *Grey-brown and smooth.*
FLOWERING TIME *Spring.*
OCCURRENCE *Woodland in S.E. Europe.*
SIMILAR SPECIES *Portugal Laurel (below), which has red-stalked leaves and longer flower clusters in summer.*

Portugal Laurel

Prunus lusitanica (Rosaceae)

An evergreen, conical to spreading tree, the Portugal Laurel is often shrubby and can have several stems from the base. The alternate, oval leaves are red-stalked, glossy, dark green above, paler below, smooth on both sides with a toothed margin. The oval fruit, to 1.2cm long, ripen from green to red then black. Subspecies *azorica* has shorter, broader leaves and shorter flower clusters.

FRAGRANT *white flowers, 1cm wide, open in long, slender clusters, to 25cm long.*

broadly spreading habit

leaf to 12cm long

HEIGHT *10m.* **SPREAD** *10m.*
BARK *Dark grey-brown and smooth.*
FLOWERING TIME *Midsummer.*
OCCURRENCE *Woodland in S.E. Europe; subsp.* azorica *is found in the Azores.*
SIMILAR SPECIES *Cherry Laurel (above), which has green-stalked leaves and shorter flower clusters in spring.*

St Lucie Cherry

Prunus mahaleb (Rosaceae)

FRAGRANT *white flowers, 2cm wide, are borne in clusters, 5cm long, in a distinctive arrangement of up to ten flowers.*

This small, deciduous tree has an open, spreading habit, and is often shrubby. Its young shoots are covered in sticky hairs. The alternate, broadly oval to almost round, shallowly toothed leaves end in short, abrupt points. They are glossy, dark green above, with hairs along the veins beneath, and turn yellow in autumn. Bowl-shaped, short-stalked white flowers open in slightly elongated clusters at the end of short, leafy shoots borne on the branches of the previous year after the foliage has emerged. The flowers have five petals and are followed by small, rounded to egg-shaped, bitter red cherries, 6mm long, that ripen to black. This cherry has given rise to several forms including some with a weeping habit or with yellow fruit.

spreading, shrubby habit

leaf to 7cm long

fruit to 1cm long

NOTE

In the Near East, the spicy seeds are used to flavour drinks, pastries, and bread; also used in the preparation of medicinal syrups.

HEIGHT *10m.*
SPREAD *10m.*
BARK *Grey-brown.*
FLOWERING TIME *Spring.*
OCCURRENCE *Woods and dry hillsides; native to C. and S. Europe.*
SIMILAR SPECIES *Sour Cherry (p.177), which has bitter black, edible fruit and is found in Europe as a cultivated plant in orchards and gardens or occasionally naturalized.*

Bird Cherry

Prunus padus (Rosaceae)

Conical when young, this deciduous tree spreads with age. The alternate leaves are toothed and end in a short point. They are matt, dark green above, and turn red or yellow in autumn. The flowers are followed by rounded or oval, bitter, glossy black fruit, 8mm long. 'Colorata', a garden selection, has purple leaves and pink flowers.

SMALL, *white, fragrant flowers are borne in slender racemes, up to 15cm long.*

leaf to 10cm long

spreading habit

flower to 1cm wide

HEIGHT *15m.* **SPREAD** *15m.*
BARK *Dark grey and smooth, rather unpleasantly scented.*
FLOWERING TIME *Spring.*
OCCURRENCE *Woodlands and river banks; native to Europe.*
SIMILAR SPECIES *Rum Cherry (p.184), which has glossy foliage.*

Peach

Prunus persica (Rosaceae)

A deciduous tree with smooth shoots, the Peach has alternate, lance-shaped, finely toothed, glossy, dark green leaves that end in a tapered point. Short-stalked, pink or sometimes white flowers, 4cm wide, are borne singly or in pairs on the bare shoots before the leaves emerge. The fruit contains a deeply-pitted, furrowed stone with a white seed. The variety *nectarina* (Nectarine) has fruit with a smooth skin.

SWEET *fleshy fruit is orange-yellow, with a red flush, and covered in velvety hairs.*

leaf to 15cm long

pink or white flowers on bare shoots

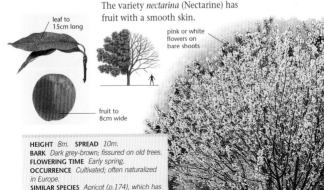

fruit to 8cm wide

HEIGHT *8m.* **SPREAD** *10m.*
BARK *Dark grey-brown; fissured on old trees.*
FLOWERING TIME *Early spring.*
OCCURRENCE *Cultivated; often naturalized in Europe.*
SIMILAR SPECIES *Apricot (p.174), which has rounded leaves and smaller fruit; Almond (p.179), which has a dry fruit.*

Sargent's Cherry

Prunus sargentii (Rosaceae)

PINK, *five-petalled flowers, 4cm wide, open in unstalked clusters of up to six.*

The young shoots of this deciduous, spreading tree are smooth and reddish. The alternate, sharply toothed leaves are oval or broadest towards the long, taper-pointed tip. They are smooth on both sides and bronzy red when young, becoming glossy, dark green above and turning orange and red in autumn. Flowers open as the young leaves emerge and are followed by rounded to oval purple-black fruit, up to 1cm long.

broadly spreading habit

leaf to 12cm long

flower to 4cm wide

HEIGHT *15m.*
SPREAD *15m.*
BARK *Red-brown with horizontal bands.*
FLOWERING TIME *Spring.*
OCCURRENCE *Cultivated (grown in parks and gardens); native to Japan.*
SIMILAR SPECIES *Japanese Cherries (p.180), which has flowers in stalked clusters.*

Rum Cherry

Prunus serotina (Rosaceae)

WHITE *flowers, up to 1cm wide, open in spreading to drooping racemes.*

This is a deciduous tree of irregular, spreading habit and slender shoots. The alternate, oval to lance-shaped leaves are edged with fine teeth and taper to a point at the tip. They are glossy, dark green above and turn yellow or red in autumn. Flower clusters are followed by round, edible fruit, up to 1cm wide, which ripen from red to black.

irregular shape

leaf to 12cm long

flower clusters up to 15cm long

HEIGHT *20m.* **SPREAD** *15m.*
BARK *Smooth, dark grey; ridged on old trees.*
FLOWERING TIME *Late spring to early summer.*
OCCURRENCE *Cultivated; native to North America.*
SIMILAR SPECIES *Bird Cherry (p.183), which has matt green leaves.*

Tibetan Cherry

Prunus serrula (Rosaceae)

Deciduous and spreading, the Tibetan Cherry has young shoots that are covered with short hairs. The alternate, lance-shaped leaves are finely toothed and end in a long, tapered point. They are matt, dark green above, with white hairs on the veins beneath. Short-stalked white flowers open singly or in clusters of up to three as the young leaves emerge. They are followed by egg-shaped fruit, up to 1cm long, that are red when ripe.

SMOOTH, *glossy red-brown bark is banded with pale, horizontal lenticels. It peels horizontally in strips.*

flower to 2cm wide

spreading habit

leaf to 10cm long

HEIGHT *15m.*
SPREAD *18m.*
BARK *Glossy red-brown and smooth; peeling in thin horizontal strips.*
FLOWERING TIME *Spring.*
OCCURRENCE *Cultivated; native to W. China.*
SIMILAR SPECIES *None – its bark is unique among the Prunus species.*

Blackthorn

Prunus spinosa (Rosaceae)

More a deciduous, thicket-forming shrub than a spreading tree, the Blackthorn has spiny shoots. The small, alternate leaves are broadest at the end, with a toothed margin. They are dark green above; hairy beneath when young. Small white flowers, about 1.5cm wide, are usually borne singly and open on the bare shoots before the leaves emerge.

ROUNDED *blue-black berries are covered with a white bloom; inedible and bitter, they are used to flavour gin.*

white flowers clothe shoots in spring

leaf to 4cm long

blue-black fruit

HEIGHT *5m.* **SPREAD** *6m.*
BARK *Dark grey-black.*
FLOWERING TIME *Spring.*
OCCURRENCE *Thickets, wood margins, and hedgerows throughout Europe.*
SIMILAR SPECIES *Cherry Plum (p.176), which flowers earlier, and has edible, plum-like fruit.*

Spring Cherry

Prunus x *subhirtella* (Rosaceae)

Deciduous and spreading, this tree has reddish young
shoots. The alternate, oval to lance-shaped leaves have
a sharply toothed margin and taper to a point at the tip.
They are bronze when they first emerge, maturing to dark
green. The flowers open in small clusters and are followed
by glossy black fruit, up to 1cm wide. The two forms most
commonly seen in gardens are 'Autumnalis', with semi-
double pale pink flowers that fade to white, and
'Autumnalis Rosea', with semi-double deep pink
flowers that fade to pale pink.

PINK *buds open into
small clusters of five-
petalled, pale pink
or white flowers,
each petal notched
at the tip.*

broadly spreading
habit

leaf to
8cm long

flower to
2cm wide

HEIGHT *6m.*
SPREAD *8m.*
BARK *Smooth and grey-brown, with horizontal bands.*
FLOWERING TIME *Late autumn, mild periods during winter,
and spring.*
OCCURRENCE *Cultivated in parks and gardens; native to Japan.*
SIMILAR SPECIES *None.*

NOTE

*This tree is a
Japanese hybrid
between the Fuji
Cherry (Prunus
incisa) and Prunus
pendula. The forms
with semi-double
flowers are popular
garden trees.*

Almond-leaved Pear

Pyrus amygdaliformis (Rosaceae)

Often shrubby, this rounded, deciduous tree has shoots that are covered in grey hairs when young and are often spine-tipped. The narrowly oval to oblong, alternate leaves are edged with small teeth or untoothed. Grey with hairs above when young, they become glossy, dark green when mature. The flowers are followed by small, rounded, yellow-brown fruit on short, stout stalks.

WHITE *flowers, up to 2.5cm wide, with five petals and orange stamens are borne in dense clusters.*

rounded habit

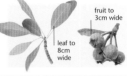

leaf to 8cm wide

fruit to 3cm wide

HEIGHT *6m.*
SPREAD *8m.*
BARK *Grey; cracking into small squares.*
FLOWERING TIME *Spring.*
OCCURRENCE *Dry, rocky places; native to the E. Mediterranean region.*
SIMILAR SPECIES *Silver Pear (p.190), which has hairier leaves.*

Callery Pear

Pyrus calleryana (Rosaceae)

This broadly conical, deciduous tree has hairy young shoots that become smooth with age. The alternate, broadly oval, sometimes wavy-edged leaves are finely toothed at the margin. They are glossy, dark green above, paler below, and turn red-purple late in autumn. The white flowers are borne in clusters of up to 12 as the young leaves emerge. 'Chanticleer' is a popular selection with a very narrow crown.

ROUNDED *to pear-shaped fruit are 2cm wide and brown dotted with white.*

broadly conical habit

flower to 2cm wide

leaf to 8cm long

HEIGHT *15m.*
SPREAD *12m.*
BARK *Dark grey; fissured and scaly with age.*
FLOWERING TIME *Spring.*
OCCURRENCE *Cultivated in parks, gardens, and streets; native to China.*
SIMILAR SPECIES *Common Pear (p.188), which has much larger fruit.*

Common Pear

Pyrus communis **(Rosaceae)**

A broadly conical to columnar, deciduous tree, the Common Pear has stout, sometimes spiny shoots. The alternate, broadly oval leaves, up to 10cm long, are hairy when young, becoming smooth as they mature. They are glossy, dark green above, with a finely toothed margin, heart-shaped base, and end in an abrupt taper-pointed tip. The white flowers with pink anthers are 2.5cm wide and are borne in clusters as the leaves emerge. They are followed by the characteristic fruit which vary in size, shape, and colour.

SWEET, *edible, round to pear-shaped fruit may be green or yellow, often flushed with red.*

broadly columnar habit

white flower clusters

NOTE

This species is thought to be a hybrid involving several European species. Along with its cultivars, it is widely grown for its edible fruit.

leaf to 10cm long

fruit to 10cm long

HEIGHT *15m.*
SPREAD *12m.*
BARK *Dark grey, cracking into small squares on older trees.*
FLOWERING TIME *Spring.*
OCCURRENCE *Known only in cultivation (grown in gardens and orchards); occasionally naturalized in Europe.*
SIMILAR SPECIES *Plymouth Pear (right) has smaller fruit and thinner, smoother bark; Wild Pear (p.190) has smaller and harder fruit.*

Plymouth Pear

Pyrus cordata (Rosaceae)

This small, deciduous tree is often shrubby and rounded, with smooth or spiny shoots. The alternate, broadly oval, glossy green leaves are finely toothed and are almost smooth when young. The 2cm-wide, white flowers are borne in clusters as the leaves emerge. The fruit are rounded to slightly more typically pear-shaped and up to 2cm long.

GREY-BROWN *bark is smoother and thinner than that of the Common Pear (left).*

small, rounded leaves

young tree

leaf to 4cm long

HEIGHT *8m.* **SPREAD** *6m.*
BARK *Grey-brown.*
FLOWERING TIME *Spring.*
OCCURRENCE *Woods and hedgerows; native to W. Europe.*
SIMILAR SPECIES *Common Pear (left), which has much larger fruit with sepals that remain attached to it.*

Snow Pear

Pyrus nivalis (Rosaceae)

The stout, usually spineless, young shoots, new leaves, and flower-bearing stalks of this deciduous, rounded tree are all densely covered with fine white hairs, giving it the common name Snow Pear. The alternate, shallowly scalloped and untoothed, oval leaves become smoother and grey-green as they mature. The white flowers, about 3cm wide, open in clusters.

ROUNDED, *yellow-green fruit become sweet when ripe; however, they are not usually eaten.*

leaf to 8cm long

rounded habit

fruit to 5cm wide

HEIGHT *8m.* **SPREAD** *8m.*
BARK *Dark grey, cracking on old trees.*
FLOWERING TIME *Spring.*
OCCURRENCE *Woods and dry slopes; native to S. and C. Europe.*
SIMILAR SPECIES *P. elaeagnifolia is a smaller, spiny tree with narrower leaves and smaller fruit.*

Wild Pear

Pyrus pyraster (Rosaceae)

WHITE *flowers, 3cm wide, with white stamens tipped with pink anthers open in clusters among the leaves.*

One of the parents of the commonly cultivated species, the Common Pear (p.188), this is a deciduous, broadly conical tree. Its shoots are often spiny and the oval to rounded leaves are alternate, finely toothed, and pointed at the tip. The white flowers are followed by small, hard, rounded to more typically pear-shaped, edible fruit. This species is sometimes not regarded as distinct from the Common Pear.

broadly conical habit

leaf to 8cm long

fruit to 4cm wide

HEIGHT *20m.* **SPREAD** *12m.*
BARK *Dark grey, cracking with age.*
FLOWERING TIME *Spring.*
OCCURRENCE *Woods and thickets; from France to E. Europe.*
SIMILAR SPECIES *Common Pear (p.188), which has larger, edible fruit; P. bourgaeana, which has smaller flowers and broader leaves.*

Silver Pear

Pyrus salicifolia 'Pendula' (Rosaceae)

SMALL, *hard, pear-shaped green fruit, 3cm long, follow the flowers.*

The shoots of this deciduous tree with weeping branches are spineless and covered with white hairs when young. The narrow, lance-shaped, untoothed leaves are tapered at both ends, with a pointed tip. They are densely covered with white hairs when young, gradually becoming smooth and dark green above. The creamy white flowers with pink anthers open in dense clusters as the leaves emerge.

weeping habit

leaf to 9cm long

flower to 2cm wide

HEIGHT *8m.*
SPREAD *8m.*
BARK *Grey-brown, cracking into square plates with age.*
FLOWERING TIME *Spring.*
OCCURRENCE *Cultivated in gardens.*
SIMILAR SPECIES *P. elaeagnifolia, which is spiny with slightly broader leaves.*

Whitebeam

Sorbus aria (Rosaceae)

A rounded, deciduous tree, the Whitebeam is conical when young. The shoots are covered with white hairs at first but become smooth with age. Arranged alternately, the oval leaves have sharply pointed teeth; they are white with hairs on both sides when young, becoming smooth and glossy, dark green above. The white flowers, up to 1.5cm wide, are followed by rounded, bright red fruit dotted with pale lenticels. *S. aria* 'Lutescens' is a commonly planted form with silvery young foliage. Some cultivated selections such as 'Majestica', have leaves 10–15cm long.

FIVE-PETALLED *flowers, with numerous white stamens, open in flattened clusters, 10cm wide.*

leaf to 12cm long

fruit to 1.5cm wide

broadly columnar habit

HEIGHT *20m.* SPREAD *20m.*
BARK *Grey and smooth; cracking and shallowly ridged with age.*
FLOWERING TIME *Late spring to early summer.*
OCCURRENCE *Widespread in woods and open areas in Europe, on well-drained, especially alkaline soils; commonly planted in parks and along streets.*
SIMILAR SPECIES *S. graeca (p.192) and Rock Whitebeam (p.196) are shrubs or small trees with leaves that are broadest above the middle.*

NOTE

In most areas, this is the commonest whitebeam with unlobed leaves. The attractive foliage and fruit has made this tree popular.

Sorbus austriaca

Sorbus austriaca (Rosaceae)

ROUNDED *fruit ripen from green to red and are spotted with conspicuous lenticels.*

Conical when young, this deciduous tree becomes rounded with age. The alternate leaves are glossy, dark green above, grey with hairs beneath. They are oval and, except at the base, edged with shallow lobes, the deepest lobes a third of the way along the leaf blade. White flowers about 1.2cm wide, with white stamens and pink anthers, are borne in clusters at the ends of the shoots.

leaf to 13cm long

fruit about 1.3cm wide

HEIGHT *10m.* **SPREAD** *8m.*
BARK *Grey and smooth.*
FLOWERING TIME *Late spring to early summer.*
OCCURRENCE *Mountain woods in E. Europe from the E. Alps to the Balkans.*
SIMILAR SPECIES *S. mougeotii (p.195) has longer leaves and the fruit has fewer lenticels.*

Sorbus graeca

Sorbus graeca (Rosaceae)

LEATHERY, *oval to nearly rounded leaves have a tapered base.*

This deciduous, rounded tree is often shrubby, with several stems. The alternate, sharply-toothed leaves are glossy, dark green above, and greenish white beneath with a dense covering of hairs. White flowers, about 1.5cm wide, each with five petals and numerous white stamens, open in dense clusters at the ends of the shoots, and are followed by rounded, bright red fruit, up to 1.2cm wide, with few, large lenticels.

shrubby habit

leaf to 9cm long

hairy underside

HEIGHT *8m.* **SPREAD** *8m.*
BARK *Grey and smooth.*
FLOWERING TIME *Late spring.*
OCCURRENCE *Woods in E. Europe.*
SIMILAR SPECIES *Rock Whitebeam (p.196) has a different distribution and fruit with numerous lenticels. S. umbellata, has shallowly lobed leaves with white hairs below.*

Swedish Whitebeam

Sorbus intermedia (Rosaceae)

A vigorous, broadly columnar to rounded, deciduous tree, the Swedish Whitebeam has hairy young shoots that soon become smooth. Except for the untoothed base, the alternate, oval leaves are edged with up to seven lobes on each side, which become smaller towards the tip, the deepest reaching about one-third of the way to the centre of the leaf. They are glossy, dark green above and grey-green with hairs beneath. Five-petalled white flowers, up to 2cm wide, are borne in dense clusters to 10cm wide in late spring. These are followed by clusters of shiny red fruit.

EGG-SHAPED *red fruit, with few lenticels are borne in dense large clusters.*

broadly columnar to rounded habit

leaf to 12cm long

fruit to 1.5cm long

NOTE

This species is commonly seen in parks and streets. It is apomictic – that is it produces identical offspring when raised from seed.

HEIGHT *15m.*
SPREAD *15m.*
BARK *Grey and smooth, cracking on old trees.*
FLOWERING TIME *Late spring.*
OCCURRENCE *Woods in N.W. Europe.*
SIMILAR SPECIES *S. mougeotii (p.195), which has rounded fruit and less deeply lobed, longer leaves as well as a very different distribution.*

Service Tree of Fontainebleau

FIVE-PETALLED, white flowers, 1.5cm wide, are borne in flattened flowerheads.

Sorbus latifolia (Rosaceae)

This broadly columnar, deciduous tree has hairy, young shoots which become glossy and smooth when mature. The alternate, broadly oval leaves, as wide as they are long, are edged with small, triangular, toothed lobes. They are glossy dark green above and covered in grey hairs beneath, turning yellow in autumn. Clusters of white flowers are followed by round, brownish red fruit, marked with conspicuous lenticels. It probably originated as a hybrid between Whitebeam (p.191) and Wild Service Tree (p.196).

fruit 1.2cm wide

leaf to 10cm long

leaves turn yellow in autumn

NOTE

Many similar trees, also intermediates between Wild Service Tree and Whitebeam or an allied species, have been described from various parts of Europe. They vary slightly in the shape of the leaves and the size and colour of the fruit.

HEIGHT *15m.* **SPREAD** *12m.*
BARK *Grey and smooth; cracking and scaly with age.*
FLOWERING TIME *Late spring.*
OCCURRENCE *Woods of S.W. Europe.*
SIMILAR SPECIES *This species is one of many in the genus that are described as apomictic, that is they produce identical offspring when grown from seed, unlike most tree species, which are variable. Some of these species are difficult to distinguish.*

Sorbus mougeotii

Sorbus mougeotii (Rosaceae)

This deciduous, rounded tree, conical when young, and sometimes a shrub, has alternate, oval leaves with shallow, toothed lobes, the deepest of which reach about one-fourth of the way to the centre of the leaf. Hairy on both sides when young, they become glossy dark green and smooth above, grey-white with hairs beneath. White flowers, 1.5cm wide, open in clusters and are followed by round, red fruit 1cm wide with few, small lenticels.

GREY-BROWN *bark is inconspicuously marked with small, horizontal lenticels.*

leaf to 10cm long

grey-white leaf underside

conical habit

HEIGHT *20m.* **SPREAD** *15m.*
BARK *Grey-brown and smooth.*
FLOWERING TIME *Late spring.*
OCCURRENCE *Mountain woods of the W. Alps and the Pyrenees.*
SIMILAR SPECIES *S. austriaca (p.192), which has relatively broader leaves and fruit with conspicuous lenticels.*

Sorbus norvegica

Sorbus norvegica (Rosaceae)

Sometimes a small tree, this deciduous species is more usually an upright to spreading shrub. The alternate broadly oval leaves, on stalks covered in grey hairs, are sharply toothed above the middle, and tapered to the base. They are glossy, dark green above and covered with white hairs beneath. White flowers open in clusters at the ends of the shoots, followed by rounded red fruit.

WHITE *flowers, about 1cm wide, have five petals and numerous white stamens.*

flower to 1cm wide

leaf to 10cm long

fruit to 1cm wide

HEIGHT *10m* **SPREAD** *10m.*
BARK *Smooth and grey.*
FLOWERING TIME *Late spring.*
OCCURRENCE *Woods of Norway and Sweden.*
SIMILAR SPECIES *Whitebeam (p.191), which is a larger tree, has larger leaves, and may be naturalized in the same area.*

Rock Whitebeam

Sorbus rupicola (Rosaceae)

TYPICALLY *found in mountainous regions of N. Europe, including Britain, where it grows in rocky places.*

This deciduous species may grow into a small, spreading tree or shrub. Widest and sharply toothed above the middle, the alternate leaves are glossy dark green above and slightly hairy at first, densely covered in white hairs beneath. White flowers, 1.5cm wide, are borne in small clusters. They are followed by rounded, red fruit, also 1.5cm wide and dotted with numerous small lenticels.

leaf to 14cm long

spreading, shrubby habit

HEIGHT *5m.* **SPREAD** *4m.*
BARK *Grey and smooth.*
FLOWERING TIME *Late spring.*
OCCURRENCE *Limestone rocks; native to N. Europe.*
SIMILAR SPECIES *Several rare Sorbus species are similar but often have lobed leaves or are much larger.*

Wild Service Tree

Sorbus torminalis (Rosaceae)

DARK *brown, the bark begins to crack into scaly plates as the tree ages.*

This deciduous tree has a broadly columnar head and glossy brown shoots that are hairy when young. The alternate, maple-like leaves are deeply cut into sharply toothed, triangular lobes. Glossy dark green above, they turn yellow, red, or purple in autumn. Small white flowers, 1.5cm wide, open in flattened heads and are followed by rounded to egg-shaped, russet-brown fruit.

ascending branches

open flower clusters

leaf to 10cm long

fruit to 1.6cm long

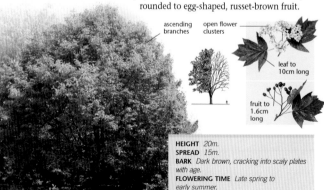

HEIGHT *20m.*
SPREAD *15m.*
BARK *Dark brown, cracking into scaly plates with age.*
FLOWERING TIME *Late spring to early summer.*
OCCURRENCE *Woods; native to Europe.*
SIMILAR SPECIES *None.*

White Poplar

Populus alba (Salicaceae)

A deciduous tree, the White Poplar is broadly columnar, spreading with age, and has young shoots that are densely covered in white hairs. The alternate leaves have rounded stalks. They have a dense layer of white hairs on both surfaces when young, but later become dark green and smooth above. On vigorous shoots, they are maple-like and deeply lobed, the larger lobes toothed, while elsewhere on the tree they have very shallow lobes. Male and female flowers are borne in drooping catkins on separate plants, the males grey with red anthers, the females green. The small green fruit capsules open to release tiny cottony seeds.

DENSE *white hairs cover the underside of leaves, which are hairy on both sides when young; they have three to five deep lobes when on vigorous shoots.*

spreading habit

white, hairy young leaves

leaf to 10cm long

NOTE
This tree, also known as Abele, produces many suckers, often at some distance from the parent. These show the lobed, maple-like leaves particularly well.

HEIGHT *30m.* **SPREAD** *20m.*
BARK *Pale grey, dark, and fissured at the base of the tree.*
FLOWERING TIME *Early spring.*
OCCURRENCE *Woods; native to Europe.*
SIMILAR SPECIES *Grey Poplar (p.198), which has unlobed leaves even on vigorous shoots, that have longer, flattened stalks and are less vividly white beneath, eventually becoming smooth; Aspen (p.200), which has flattened leaf stalks.*

Hybrid Black Poplar

Populus x *canadensis* (Salicaceae)

DROOPING *catkins of male flowers with red anthers, and green female catkins, are borne on separate trees.*

Several selections of this very vigorous, deciduous tree with a broadly columnar head, such as 'Robusta', are commonly grown. The broadly oval to nearly triangular, alternate leaves are longer on very vigorous shoots. They are often bronzy red and hairy margined when young, becoming glossy, dark green above. Tiny cottony seeds are released by small green fruit capsules.

leaf to 10cm long

pale grey bark

broadly columnar habit

HEIGHT *30m.* **SPREAD** *20m.*
BARK *Pale grey and deeply furrowed.*
FLOWERING TIME *Early spring.*
OCCURRENCE *Known only in cultivation; a hybrid between Cottonwood and Black Poplar (both right).*
SIMILAR SPECIES *Black Poplar (right), which lacks hairs on the leaf margins.*

Grey Poplar

Populus x *canescens* (Salicaceae)

PALE *grey with dark, diamond-shaped marks, the bark is dark brown and furrowed on older trees.*

This vigorous, deciduous tree spreads by suckers from the base. Its young shoots are covered in white hairs. The oval to nearly rounded leaves are toothed or only shallowly lobed. They are hairy on both sides when young, becoming smooth and dark green above, and nearly smooth beneath. Most Grey Poplars are male, bearing flowers with red anthers in pendulous catkins. This species is thought to be a hybrid between White Poplar and Aspen.

columnar habit

leaf to 8cm long

HEIGHT *30m.* **SPREAD** *20m.*
BARK *Pale grey with diamond-shaped marks; dark brown and deeply fissured on old trees.*
FLOWERING TIME *Late spring.*
OCCURRENCE *Woods and valleys of Europe.*
SIMILAR SPECIES *White Poplar (p.197), which has maple-like leaves with hairs below; Aspen (p.200), which has smooth leaves.*

Cottonwood

Populus deltoides (Salicaceae)

This is a vigorous, deciduous tree with sticky aromatic leaf buds. The broadly oval to triangular, alternate leaves have small glands where the leaf stalk meets the blade, and are edged with numerous small hairs. They are glossy green above and smooth on both sides. Flowers are borne in drooping catkins, the males with red anthers, the females green. Small green fruit open to release white, cottony seeds.

NARROW, *drooping, yellow-green female flower catkins elongate into fruit.*

broadly columnar to spreading habit

leaf to 18cm long

HEIGHT *30m.* **SPREAD** *20m.*
BARK *Pale grey and deeply furrowed.*
FLOWERING TIME *Early spring.*
OCCURRENCE *Cultivated, naturalized in Europe occasionally; native to North America.*
SIMILAR SPECIES *Hybrid Black Poplar (left), which has smaller leaves; Black Poplar (below), which has smaller, hairless leaves.*

Black Poplar

Populus nigra (Salicaceae)

The trunk of this fast growing, deciduous tree often develops large burrs. The broadly oval to triangular, alternate, finely toothed leaves have a tapered tip, and no hairs at the margin. They are bronze when young becoming glossy dark green. The flowers are in drooping catkins, the males with red anthers, the females green, on separate trees. Subsp. *betulifolia* has hairy young shoots. The selection 'Italica' is narrowly columnar with upright branches.

SMALL *green fruit, borne in catkins, open to release tiny, cottony seeds.*

broadly spreading habit

leaf to 10cm long

HEIGHT *30m.* **SPREAD** *25m.*
BARK *Dark grey and deeply fissured.*
FLOWERING TIME *Early spring.*
OCCURRENCE *River valleys of Europe; often cultivated; native to Europe.*
SIMILAR SPECIES *Hybrid Black Poplar (left) and Cottonwood (above), both of which have hairs at the edges of young leaves.*

Aspen

Populus tremula (Salicaceae)

The deciduous Aspen is conical when young, but spreads with age. Often found on poor soils, this species forms large colonies in woods, spreading by means of suckers produced by the roots. Carried on long, flattened stalks, the rounded to broadly oval leaves are edged with rounded teeth, the largest leaves borne on vigorous shoots. Bronze and hairy when young, the leaves become grey-green above, paler beneath, usually smooth on both sides, and turn yellow in autumn. The flowers are borne in drooping catkins up to 8cm long, males and females on separate trees. The male catkins are grey, while the female catkins are green. Small green fruit open to release tiny seeds that are contained within cottony white hairs.

PENDULOUS *grey male catkins, with red anthers, hang from the bare shoots in early spring.*

conical to spreading habit

leaf to 8cm long

rounded leaf

NOTE

The long, slender, flattened leaf stalks make the leaves tremble in the slightest breeze, making a rattling sound distinctive to the Aspen.

HEIGHT *20m.*
SPREAD *15m.*
BARK *Smooth and grey, darker and ridged at the base of old trees.*
FLOWERING TIME *Early spring.*
OCCURRENCE *Moist woods and hillsides all over Europe; on mountains in the south of the range.*
SIMILAR SPECIES *Grey Poplar (p.198), which has leaves covered with grey hairs beneath.*

White Willow

Salix alba (Salicaceae)

The common large waterside willow of Europe, White Willow is a vigorous, spreading, deciduous tree, often with drooping shoots. The slender, lance-shaped, finely toothed leaves end in long, tapered points. They are silky and hairy when young, becoming dark green above and blue-green below. The tiny flowers are borne in small catkins as the leaves emerge; the males are yellow, while the females are green and are borne on separate trees. Small green fruit open to release cottony seeds. The Scarlet Willow (*Salix alba* 'Britzensis') has orange-red winter shoots.

LONG, *narrow leaves show their blue-green underside with the slightest breeze blowing along the riverbank.*

spreading habit

drooping branches

leaf to 10cm long

leaves taper to fine point

yellow male catkin

green female catkin

HEIGHT *25m.* **SPREAD** *20m.*
BARK *Grey-brown, deeply fissured with age.*
FLOWERING TIME *Spring.*
OCCURRENCE *Riversides and meadows all over Europe; also commonly planted.*
SIMILAR SPECIES *Hybrid Crack Willow (p.202), which has slightly larger leaves that soon become smooth below; Crack Willow (p.203), which has larger leaves, smooth below, and shoots that snap when bent.*

(p.202)(p.203)

NOTE

The White Willow is pollarded to encourage the growth of young shoots; the wood of *Salix alba* var. *caerulea* is highly valued as it is used for making cricket bats.

Goat Willow

Salix caprea (Salicaceae)

FLOWERS *are in small catkins; the males are silvery with yellow anthers, while the females are green.*

This deciduous shrub, sometimes a small tree, is upright when young, later spreading and often branching low down or with several stems, the shoots not ridged beneath the bark. The oval, toothed, alternate leaves are hairy on both sides when young, though the grey-green uppersides becomes smooth in older trees. The flowers are borne in tiny catkins, up to 4cm long, on separate trees. Small green fruit open to release cottony seeds.

multiple stems

leaf to 10cm long

HEIGHT *10m.* **SPREAD** *8m.*
BARK *Grey and smooth; fissured on old trees.*
FLOWERING TIME *Early spring.*
OCCURRENCE *Woods and hedgerows throughout Europe.*
SIMILAR SPECIES *Eared Willow (S. aurita), which has shoots ridged beneath the bark.*

Violet Willow

Salix daphnoides (Salicaceae)

SLENDER, *finely toothed, alternate leaves are glossy, dark green above, and blue-green beneath.*

Conical when young, spreading when older, this deciduous tree has young shoots covered in a white bloom. The leaves are hairy when young becoming smooth on both sides. The flowers are borne in small, silky-hairy catkins, the males with yellow anthers, the females green, on separate trees. A small green capsule, the fruit opens to release cottony seeds.

broadly conical habit

leaf to 12cm long

HEIGHT *10m.*
SPREAD *10m.*
BARK *Dark grey and deeply fissured.*
FLOWERING TIME *Early spring.*
OCCURRENCE *Damp habitats such as moist woods in N. Europe.*
SIMILAR SPECIES *None – its bloomy shoots make it distinctive.*

Crack Willow

Salix fragilis (Salicaceae)

The twigs of this deciduous tree snap off easily from its
branches giving rise to the common name. Its alternate
leaves are silky-hairy when young, soon becoming smooth.
The small flowers lack petals and are borne in catkins on
separate trees; the males have yellow anthers, while
the females are green. Small green
fruit open to release fluffy
white seeds.

SLENDER, *toothed,
leaves end in a finely
tapered point and are
dark green above and
blue-green below.*

broadly
spreading
habit

leaf to
15cm
long

HEIGHT *15m or more.* **SPREAD** *15m.*
BARK *Dark grey and deeply fissured.*
FLOWERING TIME *Spring.*
OCCURRENCE *Riversides and meadows
throughout Europe; frequently planted.*
SIMILAR SPECIES *White Willow (p.201),
which has silky leaves and twigs that do not
snap easily.*

Bay Willow

Salix pentandra (Salicaceae)

The alternate, elliptic to narrowly ovate, slightly aromatic
dark green leaves of this deciduous, spreading tree rather
resemble those of the Bay Laurel (p.146). They are paler
beneath, finely toothed, and end in a short point. The
flowers are borne in cylindrical catkins after the leaves
emerge, the males dense and showy, with bright yellow
anthers, the females green, on separate plants. Cottony
seeds emerge from the small green fruit capsules.

CYLINDRICAL, *showy,
bright yellow male
catkins appear after
the leaves.*

leaf to 12cm
long

slender
female catkin

spreading
habit

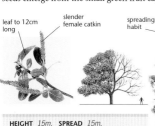

HEIGHT *15m.* **SPREAD** *15m.*
BARK *Grey-brown, with shallow fissures.*
FLOWERING TIME *Early summer.*
OCCURRENCE *Riverbanks and meadows
throughout Europe.*
SIMILAR SPECIES *Leaves have a superficial
resemblance to those of Bay Laurel (p.146),
but otherwise the tree is distinctive.*

Weeping Willow

Salix x sepulcralis 'Chrysocoma' (Salicaceae)

PALE *grey-brown, the bark is marked with shallow fissures as the tree ages.*

This deciduous, spreading tree has a rounded crown and long, pendulous yellow shoots. The alternate, slender, finely toothed leaves end in long, tapered points. Slightly silky at first, they turn smooth, bright green above and blue-green beneath. The flowers are borne in catkins and are mostly male with yellow anthers, but some are partially or completely female, with green flowers. The fruit is a small green capsule, 3mm long, which opens to release fluffy white seeds.

weeping habit

catkin to 7.5cm long

leaf to 12cm long

HEIGHT *20m.*
SPREAD *25m.*
BARK *Pale grey-brown and fissured.*
FLOWERING TIME *Spring.*
OCCURRENCE *Known only in cultivation.*
SIMILAR SPECIES *The species is a hybrid of White Willow (p.201) and S. babylonica. Although the latter was at one time grown in Europe, it has largely been replaced by Weeping Willow.*

NOTE

Among the most commonly grown weeping trees, this is a familiar sight, particularly by water. Often planted in small gardens where it becomes too large.

Empress Tree

Paulownia tomentosa (Scrophulariaceae)

The deciduous Empress Tree is broadly columnar to rounded and has very stout shoots that are hairy when young. The opposite leaves are large and oval, with a heart-shaped base and pointed tip, and often shallowly five-lobed. Dark green and velvety above, they are densely covered with sticky hairs beneath. Borne in large, upright clusters at the ends of shoots, the bell-shaped, Foxglove-like, fragrant, pale purple flowers open from buds formed the previous year.

EGG-SHAPED, *pointed fruit are borne in clusters, and ripen from green to brown.*

broadly columnar
to rounded habit

leaf to
30cm
long

flower to
5cm
long

fruit to 5cm
long

HEIGHT *15m.* **SPREAD** *12m.*
BARK *Grey and smooth with conspicuous lenticels; cracking with age to reveal broad, pale orange-brown fissures.*
FLOWERING TIME *Spring.*
OCCURRENCE *Cultivated in parks and gardens; native to China and Korea.*
SIMILAR SPECIES *Indian Bean Tree (p.114), which has leaves arranged in threes on the shoots, and very different flowers and fruit.*

NOTE

It is the clusters of pale brown, felted flower buds and persistent brown fruit that help distinguish this tree in winter.

Snowdrop Tree

Halesia monticola (Styracaceae)

The deciduous Snowdrop Tree has alternate, finely toothed, oval to oblong leaves, which end in a tapered point. Dark green above and paler beneath, they are hairy when young. The bell-shaped, white or pink-tinged flowers have four lobes and hang from the shoots in small clusters as the young leaves emerge.

WINGED *green fruit, up to 5cm long, which end in a slender point, hang downwards from the stem; they ripen to brown.*

conical to broadly columnar habit

HEIGHT *15m.* **SPREAD** *10m.*
BARK *Grey-brown; deeply furrowed on older trees.*
FLOWERING TIME *Spring.*
OCCURRENCE *Cultivated; native to S.E. USA.*
SIMILAR SPECIES *Japanese Snowbell (right), which has shorter leaves and does not have winged fruit.*

leaf to 20cm long

flower to 2cm long

Epaulette Tree

Pterostyrax hispida (Styracaceae)

Conical when young, the deciduous Epaulette Tree spreads with age. The alternate, oblong leaves have a finely toothed margin and pointed tip; they are bright green above and grey-green beneath. Small, fragrant white flowers have conspicuous stamens and are borne in large, hanging clusters up to 25cm long. The small, ribbed, brown fruit are up to 8mm long and are covered in bristly hairs.

DROOPING *clusters of bell-shaped white flowers have a distinctive fan-shaped arrangement.*

leaf to 20cm long

flower to 6mm long

spreading habit

HEIGHT *10m.* **SPREAD** *10m.*
BARK *Grey-brown, fissured.*
FLOWERING TIME *Early summer.*
OCCURRENCE *Cultivated; native to China and Japan.*
SIMILAR SPECIES *None – its fan-shaped flower clusters and bristly, ribbed fruit make it distinctive.*

Japanese Snowbell

Styrax japonicus (Styracaceae)

A deciduous tree, the Japanese Snowbell often has a short trunk and branches that emerge low down. Its alternate, oval leaves are tapered at the base and end in a pointed tip; they have a finely toothed margin. Glossy, dark green above, they may turn red or yellow in autumn. The slightly fragrant flowers have five lobes and yellow anthers and are usually white, although some forms have pink flowers. The grey-green fruit are egg-shaped and about 1cm long.

BELL-SHAPED, *white or pink-tinged flowers hang from slender stalks in clusters beneath the branches.*

broadly spreading habit

leaf to 10cm long

flower to 1.5cm long

HEIGHT *10m.* **SPREAD** *15m.*
BARK *Dark grey-brown and smooth; brownish fissures and ridges on old trees.*
FLOWERING TIME *Early summer.*
OCCURRENCE *Cultivated (in parks and gardens); native to China, Japan, and Korea.*
SIMILAR SPECIES *Snowdrop Tree (left), which has winged fruit and longer leaves.*

Tamarix africana

Tamarix africana (Tamaricaceae)

Spreading and deciduous, often branching low or a shrub, this species has scale-like, bright green leaves. The slender young shoots are densely covered with tiny, scale-like leaves up to 4mm long. The tiny flower petals often persist after flowering. The fruit are inconspicuous. One of several, mostly uncommon species of *Tamarix* in Europe, it can be rather difficult to distinguish.

TINY *five-petalled white or pale pink flowers are borne in dense, slender clusters.*

spreading habit

flower clusters to 5cm long

HEIGHT *7m.* **SPREAD** *6m.*
BARK *Dark purple to black.*
FLOWERING TIME *Spring, from the old shoots, sometimes summer from new shoots.*
OCCURRENCE *Coastal salt marshes; native to S.W. Europe, naturalized in S. England.*
SIMILAR SPECIES T. parviflora *(below), which has flowers with four petals.*

Tamarix parviflora

Tamarix parviflora (Tamaricaceae)

The long and arching branches of this tree or shrub are often produced low down. Its slender young shoots are densely covered with tiny, scale-like, bright green leaves up to 4mm long. Borne in clusters from the previous year's shoots, the flowers are only 2mm long. The fruit are inconspicuous.

spreading to shrubby habit

FOUR-PETALLED, *tiny, pale pink flowers are borne in dense, very slender clusters.*

flower cluster to 5cm long

HEIGHT *5m.* **SPREAD** *6m.*
BARK *Brown to purple-brown.*
FLOWERING TIME *Spring.*
OCCURRENCE *Hedgerows and river banks; native to S.E. Europe, it is planted and sometimes naturalized elsewhere.*
SIMILAR SPECIES T. africana *(above), which has flowers with five petals.*

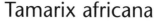

Stewartia pseudocamellia

Stewartia pseudocamellia (Theaceae)

Conical when young, this deciduous tree becomes broadly columnar with age. The oval, finely toothed leaves end in short, tapered points. They are dark green and smooth above, smooth or hairy beneath, and turn yellow, orange, or red in autumn. The fruit is a woody, red-brown capsule, about 2cm long. This species is very distinctive in its bark and flowers, the latter falling intact from the tree. Like the related Camellia, this tree only grows in areas with lime-free soil.

CAMELLIA-LIKE *and white, each flower has numerous bright yellow stamens, and five wavy-edged petals joined at the base.*

conical to broadly
columnar habit

leaf to 10cm
long

flower
6cm
wide

red-
brown
bark

HEIGHT *15m.* **SPREAD** *10m.*
BARK *Red-brown, flaking conspicuously to leave grey and pink patches.*
FLOWERING TIME *Summer.*
OCCURRENCE *Cultivated in parks and gardens; native to Japan and Korea.*
SIMILAR SPECIES *None – some other species in this genus are occasionally grown in gardens but much less commonly.*

NOTE

Closely related to the more common evergreen, shrubby camellias seen in gardens, this tree is only found in areas with acidic soils.

Small-leaved Lime

Tilia cordata (Tiliaceae)

The Small-leaved Lime is a large, deciduous tree with a broadly columnar head. The rounded, alternate leaves have a sharply toothed margin, are heart-shaped at the base, and end in a short, abruptly tapered point. They are dark green above and blue-green beneath, turning yellow in autumn. The leaves are smooth below with conspicuous tufts of brown hairs in the leaf axils. The rounded, grey-green fruit are about 1.2cm long. Unlike other limes, this tree is usually without or with few suckers at the base.

FRAGRANT *pale yellow flowers, 2cm wide, open in small, hanging clusters at the base of which are single, conspicuous yellow-green bracts.*

broadly columnar habit

leaf to 8cm long

HEIGHT *30m.*
SPREAD *20m.*
BARK *Smooth and grey; furrowed with age.*
FLOWERING TIME *Summer.*
OCCURRENCE *Woods, often on limestone, throughout Europe.*
SIMILAR SPECIES *Common Lime (right), which has leaves with green undersides; Broad-leaved Lime (right), which has leaves covered with soft hairs beneath.*

NOTE

This species is one of the parents of the Common Lime (right). Several selections of narrow or conical habit are grown in gardens.

Common Lime

Tilia x europaea (Tiliaceae)

A hybrid between Small-leaved Lime (left) and Broad-leaved Lime (below), this vigorous and large, deciduous tree is broadly columnar in habit, and is often seen with numerous suckers at the base. The rounded to broadly oval, alternate leaves are sharply toothed and end in a short point. They are dark green above, green and smooth beneath except for tufts of hairs in the axils of the veins.

EGG-SHAPED *grey-green fruit are 1.2cm long, and similar to those of the Small-leaved Lime (left).*

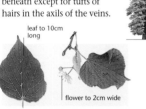

broadly columnar habit

leaf to 10cm long

flower to 2cm wide

HEIGHT *40m.* **SPREAD** *20m.*
BARK *Grey-brown, shallow fissures with age.*
FLOWERING TIME *Early spring.*
OCCURRENCE *Woodlands of Europe; also cultivated.*
SIMILAR SPECIES *Small-leaved Lime (left), has blue-green leaf undersides; Broad-leaved Lime (below), has hairy leaf undersides.*

Broad-leaved Lime

Tilia platyphyllos (Tiliaceae)

One of the parents of Common Lime (above), this large, deciduous tree, with a broadly columnar head, may sometimes have many suckers at the base. Its young shoots are usually covered with soft white hairs. The alternate leaves are dark green above, paler beneath, and usually softly hairy on both sides. The fragrant flowers and fruit are similar to those of Small-leaved Lime (left).

ROUNDED *to broadly oval, the leaves are sharply toothed and end in a short point.*

leaf to 12cm long

leaves turn yellow in autumn

flower to 2cm wide

HEIGHT *30m.* **SPREAD** *20m.*
BARK *Grey, shallowly fissured with age.*
FLOWERING TIME *Summer.*
OCCURRENCE *Woods of Europe.*
SIMILAR SPECIES *Common Lime (above), and Small-leaved Lime (left), both of which have leaves with smoother undersides, except for the tufts of hair in the axils.*

Silver Lime

Tilia tomentosa (Tiliaceae)

ROUNDED *leaves are often unequal at the base, and end in a short, tapered point. Woody and grey-green, the fruit are rounded to egg-shaped.*

The young shoots of the Silver Lime have a dense covering of silvery hairs, hence its common name. It is a deciduous tree with a broadly columnar habit. The alternate leaves are dark green above and are covered with silvery hairs beneath; leaf margins are sharply toothed and sometimes slightly lobed. The very fragrant, five-petalled yellow flowers are borne in clusters, up to ten together, at the base of which is a conspicuous pale green bract. The green fruit are up to 1.2cm long.

broadly columnar habit

leaf to 12cm long

flower to 2cm wide

green bract

NOTE

The species is frequently planted in streets and parks. Weeping Silver Lime (T. tomentosa 'Petiolaris'), with long-stalked leaves and drooping branches, is particularly common.

HEIGHT *25m.*
SPREAD *15m.*
BARK *Grey; growing shallowly fissured with age.*
FLOWERING TIME *Mid- to late summer.*
OCCURRENCE *Woods of S.E. Europe.*
SIMILAR SPECIES *None – it is the silvery hairs of the leaves and shoots that distinguish Silver Lime from other European species.*

Nettle Tree

Celtis australis (Ulmaceae)

This is a deciduous tree with a broadly columnar to spreading head. The alternate, oval leaves have a sharply-toothed margin, are three-veined and slender-pointed at the tip, and often oblique at the base. Tiny, green, and without petals, the flowers open singly or in small clusters in the axils of the leaves as these are expanding, the males and females separate on the same tree. The rounded, berry-like, edible fruit, up to 1cm wide, ripen from green to black.

NARROW *oval leaves are dark green and rough to the touch above, grey-green and softly hairy beneath.*

broadly columnar head

leaf to 15cm long

NOTE

This tree thrives in warm, dry areas of Europe, and can commonly be seen planted in streets and squares in the Mediterranean region.

HEIGHT *20m.*
SPREAD *20m.*
BARK *Pale grey and smooth.*
FLOWERING TIME *Spring.*
OCCURRENCE *Woods and thickets in dry, rocky areas of S. Europe.*
SIMILAR SPECIES *Some species of elms, but these lack the three-veined leaves and berry-like fruit of Nettle Tree.*

Wych Elm

Ulmus glabra (Ulmaceae)

TINY *flowers with red anthers open on the bare shoots in late winter before the leaves emerge.*

Conical when young, this large, deciduous tree develops a rounded head with age and has rough young shoots. The alternate, oval leaves have unequal halves, with sharp teeth that are larger towards the tip. They are dark green and very rough above, with a short stalk. The flowers are followed by winged green fruit. Dutch Elm *(U. x hollandica)* is a hybrid between Wych Elm and Field Elm.

rounded head

fruit to 2cm long

leaf to 15cm long

HEIGHT *30m.*
SPREAD *25m.*
BARK *Grey and smooth, becoming ridged in old trees.*
FLOWERING TIME *Late winter.*
OCCURRENCE *Woods and hedgerows throughout Europe.*
SIMILAR SPECIES *None.*

White Elm

Ulmus laevis (Ulmaceae)

SLENDER-STALKED, *winged, green fruit to 1.2cm long, are edged with hairs.*

The young shoots on this deciduous tree are covered in soft grey hairs. The alternate, broadly oval to rounded leaves are sharply toothed and very unequal at the base. They are dark green and smooth or slightly rough above, and grey with hairs beneath. Tiny flowers with red anthers open on bare shoots, and are followed by the fruit.

leaf to 12cm long

open, spreading head

HEIGHT *30m.* **SPREAD** *25m.*
BARK *Grey-brown and smooth, becoming furrowed with age.*
FLOWERING TIME *Late winter.*
OCCURRENCE *Wooded valleys in C. and E. Europe.*
SIMILAR SPECIES *None – its slender-stalked, pendulous, white-haired fruit make it distinct.*

Field Elm

Ulmus minor (Ulmaceae)

Like other elms, the alternate, oval leaves of the Field Elm are very unequal at the base and have sharply toothed margins. They are glossy green and smooth above, paler beneath with hairs only on the veins. The tree is deciduous, with a columnar head and has smooth young shoots. The fruit, to 1.5cm long, are green-winged with the seed positioned above the middle.

FLOWERS *in tiny clusters have red anthers and open on the bare shoots.*

columnar habit

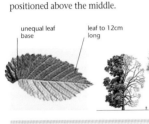

unequal leaf base

leaf to 12cm long

HEIGHT *30m.* **SPREAD** *20m.*
BARK *Pale grey and smooth when young, becoming fissured with age.*
FLOWERING TIME *Late winter.*
OCCURRENCE *Woods, thickets, and hedgerows throughout Europe.*
SIMILAR SPECIES *English Elm (below), which has hairs covering the leaf underside.*

English Elm

Ulmus procera (Ulmaceae)

This deciduous tree with a broadly columnar head usually has suckers at the base, and shoots which can become corky when a few years old. The broadly oval to rounded alternate leaves are sharply toothed with a very unequal base. They are dark green and rough to the touch above and hairy beneath. Winged, green fruit, 1.5cm long, have seeds positioned above the middle.

DENSE *clusters of tiny flowers with red anthers open on the bare shoots.*

broadly columnar habit

flowers open on bare shoots

leaf to 10cm long

HEIGHT *30m.* **SPREAD** *20m.*
BARK *Grey and smooth when young, becoming furrowed with age.*
FLOWERING TIME *Late winter.*
OCCURRENCE *Woods, fields, and hedgerows of W. Europe; often planted.*
SIMILAR SPECIES *Field Elm (above), which has leaves smooth on the upper side.*

Cretan Zelkova

Zelkova abelicea (Ulmaceae)

SMOOTH, *grey-brown bark has conspicuous narrow bands of lenticels.*

Often branching low and sometimes shrubby, this deciduous, spreading tree has slender young shoots covered in white hairs. The short-stalked, narrowly oval, alternate leaves have four or five teeth on each side. They are dark green above, paler and hairy beneath. The flowers are tiny and green; while the males are in clusters, the females are usually borne singly and followed by small, rounded fruit about 5mm wide.

low branches

leaf to 4cm long

HEIGHT *6m.*
SPREAD *8m or more.*
BARK *Grey and smooth.*
FLOWERING TIME *Spring.*
OCCURRENCE *Rocky mountain slopes of Crete.*
SIMILAR SPECIES *Caucasian Elm (below), which has larger leaves with more teeth.*

Caucasian Elm

Zelkova carpinifolia (Ulmaceae)

OBLONG, *dark green leaves are edged with usually 9–11 pairs of triangular teeth.*

This is a deciduous, columnar tree with a short trunk and a dense, oval head of numerous, ascending branches. The short-stalked, alternate leaves are dark green and rough above with hairs along the veins beneath, and turn orange-brown in autumn. The flowers are tiny and green, with the males in clusters; usually borne singly, the female flowers are followed by small, rounded fruit 6mm wide.

leaf to 10cm long

broadly columnar habit

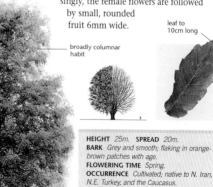

HEIGHT *25m.* **SPREAD** *20m.*
BARK *Grey and smooth; flaking in orange-brown patches with age.*
FLOWERING TIME *Spring.*
OCCURRENCE *Cultivated; native to N. Iran, N.E. Turkey, and the Caucasus.*
SIMILAR SPECIES *Cretan Zelkova (above), which has smaller leaves with fewer teeth.*

Glossary

Many of the terms defined here are illustrated in the general introduction (pp. 8–11). Words in *italics* are defined elsewhere in the glossary.

ALTERNATE Borne singly, in two vertical rows or spirally.

ANTHER The male part of the flower that bears the pollen.

ARIL A fleshy, often brightly coloured, coat on a seed.

AURICLED With small, ear-like lobes.

AXIL The angle between two structures, such as the leaf and stem or the *midrib* and a small vein.

BIPINNATE Twice *pinnate*, i.e. with the divisions themselves pinnately divided.

BLOOMY Covered with a thin blue-white layer which can be rubbed off.

BRACT A small, leaf-like structure found at the base of flowers or in the *cone* of a conifer.

BURR A woody outgrowth on the trunk of some trees.

BUTTRESSED With a fluted or swollen trunk that aids stability in shallow rooting conditions.

CATKIN An unbranched and often pendulous flower cluster of a single sex.

COLUMNAR Taller than broad, with parallel sides.

COMPOUND Describes a leaf divided into *leaflets*.

CONE The fruiting structure of conifers.

CONICAL Widest at the bottom, tapering towards the top.

CULTIVAR A selection made by humans and maintained in cultivation.

DECIDUOUS Describes a tree that is leafless for part of the year (usually winter).

DOUBLE FLOWER Describes a flower with more petals than in the normal wild state, and with few, if any, *stamens*.

EVERGREEN Describes a tree that always bears leaves.

FORM Any variant of a *species*.

GENUS A category in classification consisting of a group of closely related *species*, and denoted by the first part of the scientific name, e.g. Pinus in Pinus pinea.

HABIT The shape of a plant.

HERBACEOUS Non-woody, dying back at the end of the growing season and overwintering by means of undeground rootstocks.

HYBRID A cross between two different *species*.

LEADING SHOOT The *terminal* shoot of a main branch.

LEAFLET One of the divisions that make up a *compound* leaf.

LENTICEL A small pore found on shoots and fruit through which air can pass.

MIDRIB The primary, usually central, vein of a leaf or *leaflet*.

NATIVE Occurring naturally in a particular region.

NATURALIZED A non-native plant, introduced by human activity into a region, and now forming self-sustaining populations in the wild.

OBOVATE Egg-shaped, broadest above the middle.

OPPOSITE Borne in pairs on opposite sides of the stem.

OVATE Egg-shaped, broadest towards the base.

PALMATELY COMPOUND Fan-shaped and divided into *leaflets*.

PANICLE An elongated, branched flower cluster, with stalked flowers.

PEA-LIKE Describes a flower structure typical of members of the Pea family, with the *sepals* fused into a short tube, and usually with an erect upper petal, two wing petals, and two lower petals forming a keel.

PERSISTENT Not falling, but remaining attached to the plant.

PINNATE Describes a *compound* leaf with the *leaflets* arranged as in a feather. Pinnately lobed leaves have lobes, rather than leaflets, arranged in this manner.

RACEME An elongated, unbranched flower cluster, with stalked flowers.

SELECTION see **CULTIVAR**.

SEMI-EVERGREEN With few leaves retained over winter.

SEPAL The usually green parts of a flower outside of the petals, collectively called the calyx.

SIMPLE Undivided.

SPECIES A classification category defining a group of similar and usually interbreeding plants, e.g. Scots Pine (Pinus sylvestris) is one species.

STAMEN Male part of a flower, composed of an *anther*, normally borne on a stalk (filament).

STIGMA The female part of the flower that receives the pollen.

STIPULE A leaf-like organ at the base of a leaf stalk.

SUBSPECIES (abbrev. **SUBSP.**) A category of classification, below species, defining a group within a species, isolated geographically but able to interbreed with others of the same species.

SUCKERS Shoots arising from below the soil at the base of a tree.

TEPALS Sepals and petals when they look alike.

TERMINAL Located at the end of a shoot, stem, or other organ.

VARIEGATED Having more than one colour; usually used to describe leaves.

VARIETAS (abbrev. **VAR.**) A naturally occurring variant of a species.

Index

Acknowledgments

Dorling Kindersley would like to thank Bridget Lloyd-Jones for her help with picture administration and editing, Erin Richards for additional administrative assistance.

PICTURE CREDITS
Picture librarians : Richard Dabb, Claire Bowers

Abbreviations key: a = above, b = bottom, c = centre, f = far, l = left, r = right, t = top.

The publishers would like to thank the following for their kind permission to reproduce the photographs:

A D Schilling: 10 br; 11 bc; 12 ca; 17 tr; 23 tr; 27 bl, tr; 29 tr; 34 tl; 36 ca; 37 bcr, cfr, tr; 38 cfl; 39 cfr; 40 cfl; 41 ca; 44 tl; 47 bcl; 48 cal, cfl; 58 bcr; 60 cla, cal; 62 tl; 71 cfr; 88 tl; 99 tr; 102 tl; 104 tl; 110 tl; 114 tl; 115 tr; 117 cb; 118 cb; 120 cfl, tl, 126 tl; 127 cfr; 138 tr; 146 cfl; 148 tl, bl; 150 bcr; 151 tr; 153 tr; 178 tl; 187 tl; 203 cfr.
Alan Outen: 177 tr; 31 tr.
Alistair Duncan: 72 cfl; 183 cfr.
Andreas Stieglitz: 17 tr, cla, cra.
Andrew Beckett: 94 tl.
Andrew Butler: 62 cal; 92 bl; 111 car, tr; 127 bl; 147 bcl; 149 cla, tr; 159 bcr; 185 tr; 216 bl, cfl.
Andrew de Lory: 76 car, cfl.
Ardea: 97 cfr; 166 bl.
B Borrell Casals: 125 cla; 154 cal; 183 br.
Bob Gibbons: 179 tr.
C Andrew Henley: 41 tr.
Chris Gibson: 1c; 10 bcr; 11 br; 12 bl; 13 bcl; 14 cra; 15 tr; 16 bcl; 18 br; 19 cr, tr; 22 cra; 28 cfl; 35 bcr, cal, car, cfr, tr; 38 cra, tl; 39 cla, tr; 42 car; 46 tl; 55 car, tr; 59 tr; 60 bcl, br, cfl, cra, tl; 66 tl; 69 tr; 71 cla; 73 bl; 74 tl; 75 cfl; 76 bcl; 82 cb; 89 cb; tr; 90 c, br; 91 ca; 92 tl; 93 tr; 95 cfr, cla; 97 cra; 100 tl; 110 cfl; 115 cla; 116 car; 119 cal; 121 ca; 124 ca, tl; 126 bl, cfl; 127 car; 128 tl; 129 cb, tr; 131 bl; 134 br, cfl; 137 cb, tr; 139 tr; 140 bcl; 142 bcl; 144 br; 146 tl; 147 cfr, tr; 150 cal; 151 cfr; 152 bcl; 154 car; 156 bcl, cfl; 157 cal, cfr; 159 cfr; 160 tl; 161 bcr, car, cfr, tr; 163 cfr; 166 cfl; 167 tr; 168 tl; 171 car; 173 tr; 175 tr; 176 tl; 179 br, tr; 181 br, cal, tr; 183 tr; 185 bl; 190 ca; 191 tr; 192 cfl; 196 car; 199 bcl, cfr; 200 tl; 202 tl; 203 tr; 204 ca; 205 ca, tr; 208 cal, tl; 209 tr; 210 ca; 211 cfr; 215 bl, car.
Clive Boursnell: 67 cla; 145 car; 211 bl.
David Dixon: 179 cra.
David Hosking: 142 tl, cla; 184 bcl; 214 br.
Deni Bown: 61 cal; 156 tl; 210 bl.
Derek Hall: 142 cra.
E&D Hosking: 94 br; 157 bl; 182 br; 194 tl.
Eric Crichton: 42 tl; 48 tl; 73 cfr; 169 tr.
F Collect: 199 tr.
FLPA: 154 bcl, cal; 166 cbr.
Frank Lane Picture Agency, Leo Batten: 186 tl.
Garden Picture Library Howard Rice: 87 tr.
Heinz Schneider: 10 cfl; 47 ca; 54 bcl; 55 car; 72 bcl, cbr, crb.
Henriette Kress: 86 cra, tl.
Howard Rice: 12 br; 18 car; 31 tr; 50 cl; 157 tr; 199 cla, cra.
Ingmar Holmasen: 166 tl, cla; cra; 192 cra; 194 bl; 195 tr.
Jens Schou: 2; 3; 4; 5; 8 cbl; 11 tc; 12 bcl; 14 cal; tl; 15 ca; 17 cfl; 20 cl, tl; 22 bcl, cfl; 23 bl, cfr; 26 cl; 30 bcl, cfl, cra, tl; 32 tl; 33 cb; 34 br, cfl; 58 br; 68 cfl; 72 cal, tl; 75 bl; 86 bl, cal, cfl, cla; 103 tr; 111 bl; 142 cfl; 171 tr; 175 ca; 192 cb; 193 tr; 195 bl, cfr.

John Ferro Sims: 87 bc.
John Fielding: 32 cl.
John Glover: 8 tcl; 36 tl; 40 cal; 42 cfl; 53 tr; 68 bcl; 119 cfr; 163 tr; 169 cfr; 184 tl.
Joseph Strauch: 10 bl; 144 cfl; 31 cr.
Juliette Wade: 28 br; 29 ca; 51 car; 57 cr; 119 tr.
Jurgen & Christine Sohns: 62 clb.
Justyn Willsmore: 12 bcr; 58 ca; 119 bcr; 158 ca; 180 tl, ca; 181 bcr; 184 cal.
Keith Rushforth: 71 tr; 80 clb; 92 cra; 107 cfr; 184 cal; 190 cla; 192 tl, cal; 198 tl; 203 br.
KW Fink: 61 bl.
Life Science Images: 83 cfr.
Mr Lloyd-Jones: 154 cla.
Mark Newman: 83 bl.
Martin B Withers: 97 bl; 178 bl; 202 clb; br.
Matthew Ward: 127 tr.
Maurice Nimmo: 174 bl.
Michael L Charters: 208 clb, br.
Michael Rose: 82 car; 154 bl.
Mike J Thomas: 214 cra.
Mike Slater: 174 clb; John R Seiler: 66bl; 71 br; 126 cra; 177 c.
Natural Image Bob Gibbons: 83 crb; 86 tl; 143 bl; 154 tl; 160 cra, clb, bl; 186 c; 192 bcl; 208 cra, bl; 214 tl, clb, bl; 215 tr.
Nature Photographers Ltd: 82 tl.
Neil Fletcher: 10 c, cr, cbr; 11 bcl, tr, cal, cra, bl, cla; 13 car, cfr, tr; 14 br; 16 cfl, cra, tl; 17 cr; 18 cfl; 21 bl, cal, car, cfr, cla, cfr, tr; 22 tl; 23 car; 24 cbl, cra, tl; 26 tl; 27 cfr; 28 tl; 37 car, clb; 38 bcl, cfr; 39 bl; 40 cbl; 42 bcl; 43 ca, tr; 44 cr; 45 bl, car, tr; 46 ca; 47 bcr, bl; 48 br; 49 bcr, cfr, tr; 50 tl; 51 bcr, cfr, tr; 52 cl, tl; 53 cr; 54 cfl, cra, crb, tl; 55 bl, br, cfr; 56 bcl, cfl, crb, tl; 57 tr; 59 bcr, cfr; 60 crb; 61 car; 63 ca, cbl, cbr, tr; 64 cr, tl; 65 ca, tr; 66 cal; 67 cfr, cra, tr; 68 tl; 70 cbl, cfl, cra, tl; 72 cra; 73 car; 75 car, tl; 76 tl; 77 cb, tr; 78 cb, tl; 79 cb, tr; 80 bcl, car, cb, cfl; 81 ca, tr; 83 car, tr; 84 bcr, car, tl; 86 crb; 91 tr; 93 cr; 94 cfl; 95 cra, tr; 96 cl, tl; 97 cal; 98 ca, tl; 99 car; 101 ca, tr; 102 bl, car, cfl; 103 bl, car, cfr; 104 bl, cal, cbr, cla; 106 ca, tl; 107 bl; 108 ca, tl; 109 bl, br, ca, cfr, tr; 111 cfr; 112 cl, tl; 113 bl, car, cfr, tr; 114 cal, cfl; 115 bl, car, cfr; 116 br, cfl, clb, tl; 118 car, cfl, tl; 119 cra; 120 bcr, cal; 121 tr; 122 bcl, bl, cal, cbl, cfl, cra, tl; 123 cal, clb, tr; 125 cb, cfr; 129 cla; 130 cr, tl; 131 car, cfr, tr; 132 bcl, cal, cfl, tl; 133 tr; 134 cal, clb, tl; 135 bcl, car, cfr, crb, tr; 136 bl, car, cfl, tl; 138 bl, car, cfl, cla; 139 ca, cbl; 140 car, cfl, tl; 141 ca, tr; 143 cbr, cfr,cla, tr; 144 cal, tl; 145 br, cb, cfr, tr; 146 bcl, cal; 148 cb; 150 cfl, tl; 151 br ,cla; 152 ca, cfl; 153 cla; 154 cbr, cfl; 155 bcr, car, cfr, clb, tr; 156 car; 159 cla, tr; 162 cal, car, cb, cfl, cra, tl; 163 bl, cla; 164 ca, tl; 165 ca, tr; 167 cb; 168 bcr, cal, car, cfl; 169 car, cb; 170 ca, tl; 171 bl, cfr; 172 bcl, car, tl; 173 ca; 176 ca; 178 cal, car, cfr; 179 cfr; 181 cal, cfr; 183 cal; 185 cbr, cfr, cla; 187 br, car, cfr, cla; 188 tl; 189 bl, ca, cfr, cra, crb, tr; 190 bl, cfl; 191 cb; 193 cr; 195 car, cla, tr; 196 bl, cfl; 197 ca, tr; 198 bl, car, cfl; 200 cb; 201 ca, tr; 202 ca, cal; 203 car; 204 tl; 206 br, car, cfl, tl; 207 ca; 209 cb; 211 cra, tr; 212 ca, tl; 213 tr; 216 cal, cla, tl.
Oxford Scientific Films Deni Brown: 85 tr, c; 125 tr.
Roger Wilmshurst: 74 c.
RP Lawrence: 215 cfr.
Silvertris: 154 crb.
Steven Still: 33 tr.
Steven Wooster: 174 car, tl.
Wardene Weisser: 83 br.
All other images © Dorling Kindersley.